May 1, 1981

Cisco!

Get ready for Walt
Forsiak's next visit
to Bodega!

Best wishes from
Bob Burger

THE
JUG WINE
BOOK

THE
JUG WINE
BOOK

Robert Burger

STEIN AND DAY/*Publishers*/New York

In heaven it is always autumn.
—Chaucer

ACKNOWLEDGMENTS

I would like to acknowledge the help of Joan Cashel, Fred Cherry, Jack and Sandy Dunne, and Walter Forsiak, whose dedication is the best any book could have.

First published in 1980
Copyright © 1980 by Robert Burger
All rights reserved
Designed by David Miller
Printed in the United States of America
Stein and Day/*Publishers*/Scarborough House
Briarcliff Manor, N.Y. 10510

Library of Congress Cataloging in Publication Data

Burger, Robert E
     The jug wine book.

     Bibliography: p. 144
     1. Wine and wine making.   I. Title.
TP548.B94   641.2'2   79-65110
ISBN 0-8128-2689-2
ISBN 0-8128-6032-2 pbk.

Contents

FOREWORD   7

1. A Question of Taste   9

2. Everyday Wines   20

3. Jugs Ordinaire   63

4. A Sunday Kind of Jug   68

5. House Wines   73

6. Touring the Jug Wine Country   84

7. Jug Wines in the Kitchen   103

8. Improving the Breed   111

APPENDIX

I. Index of Domestic and Imported Jug Wines,
with Capsule Evaluations   118

II. Newsletters, Booklets, Slides, Tapes, Tours,
Clubs, Groups, and Products Related to Wine   134

III. The Wine Growing Regions of California   138

IV. Wine Labeling Regulations   139

V. Annotated Bibliography   144

INDEX   147

Foreword

This book is the product of an evolution of American wine making. What we once disparaged as jug wines have found their way into elegant homes as well as onto picnic tables, and to wine tastings as well as into punch bowls. They appear now in magnums and fifths as well as in jugs. For these *everyday* wines are no longer defined by the shape or size of a container, but by their value.

It would have been thought unnecessary to devote an entire book to jug wines even as recently as the late 1960s. But the quality and range of these wines have increased prodigiously, so much so that enologists claim that jug wines are now superior to premium wines made in California only a couple of decades ago.

This book is primarily a guide to the best values in everyday wines and to your full enjoyment of them at home, while eating out, or while touring. It also explores the romance and adventure of wine appreciation. Though its immediate value lies in its practicality, I hope that, like a sound wine, this book will be opened years from now and be found mellow and mature.

ROBERT BURGER
Berkeley, 1979

1

A Question of Taste

... helping ourselves to wine from the grass-covered flask; it swung in a metal cradle and you pulled the neck of the flask down with the forefinger and the wine, clear red, tannic and lovely, poured out into the glass held with the same hand. ...

—Ernest Hemingway, *A Farewell to Arms*

The house wine of Italy, they say, is Frascati—a tart but clear descendant of Hemingway's jug. In the first two decades of this century wine was generally big, tannic, *tart.* They didn't call them jug wines, because that's what most people drank, but then in the natural evolution of things wine became precious and refined and people started to believe that what they had always drunk was common. And the jugs that the common man's wine came in became the name for the wine.

The spirit of jug wines, which this book is all about, is Italian—or at least Mediterranean. One need only look to the house wines of the United States to confirm this impression: the Gallos, the Giumarras, the Cribaris, the Franzias, the d'Agostinis, the Guastis, the Pedroncellis, the DiGiorgios, the Sebastianis, the Petris, the Romas, and a dozen other household names among wine drinkers are evidence enough of the impact of the Italian makers on how we "help ourselves to wine."

Our taste, we are told, is informed by psychology as well as by sweet, bitter, acid, and salt—the four physiological indicators. It seems that history may also play a role. The word "jug," itself, demeans its contents, so easily have we forgotten that large containers were once the accepted receptacles of the vintner's art. Before Prohibition, the California wine makers brought their product to shops and restaurants in small barrels and glass containers of various sizes to be exchanged for their empty counterparts, in much the same way as small family dairies brought their milk in cans. My mother performed this delivery function for her family in the years after World War I. And my good friend Salvatore C.J. Fusco was, at the same time, driving a wagon through the streets of San Francisco with Louis Martini delivering Martini's father's wine in bulk. Now the market for the "fussier" wines is such that the Louis Martini label appears only on fifths and a few magnums.

At the very start, then, it should be clear that I feel the good name of jug wines needs to be reaffirmed against their onetime fall from critical favor; and that a large part of this book will be devoted to restoring that balance. *Mirabile dictu,* the quality of jug wines has undergone a resurgence by an accident of economics: a tremendous overplanting of grape vines in the early seventies by businessmen looking for a tax dodge flooded the market with young grapes that couldn't be turned into raisins. From a high of about $1100 a ton, the price of cabernet plunged to $500. At the same time, drinking tastes were changing, too. Moving away from "heavier" drinks like Kentucky sour mash and Guinness Stout, diet-conscious patrons of bars and parties (it would be a distortion to call them "drinkers") started asking for things that were white: light scotches, watery beers, white wines, and, eventually, Perrier water. The white wines of distinction were victims of a hit-and-run accident: they could be as vigorous and full as any Beaujolais or Gamay, but lighter became better in the minds of the drinkers. And so the flood of premium grapes and the whims of consumers unleashed an embarrassment of riches for red wine lovers.

The inevitable question in any assessment of wine must be "How does it taste?" It would seem that this giant poll of consumer preferences has rendered the verdict that white wines taste better. White wines of almost any character at all. Yet this poll *has* performed a fine public function. Once we were inundated by critics who proclaimed, "Drink what you like." Now, at least, we know we must define the categories of wine very carefully before we accept our first impressions as the authority for taste.

"About tastes there is no disputing" is the rule against which we must measure any discussion of the taste of wine. *De gustibus.* Yet an uneducated wine drinker is like a child. It's silly to tell a child "Eat what you like." The trouble is, the word *taste* means two quite different things.

TASTE: EDUCATED OR IN YOUR MOUTH

In a recent newsletter of one of the country's premier wine importers, this was the description of some French Cote d'Or: "The 76s are now looking very withdrawn and sullen." *San Francisco Chronicle* columnist Herb Caen commented, "When they turn surly, grab your Cote and head for the d'Or."

This is the *reductio ad absurdum* of descriptions of taste—taste on the palate. And this is why most wine *tastings* can be so misleading. *The thing you're tasting isn't defined.*

If you've ever read a wine newsletter or a summary of a wine tasting in a newspaper, you'll appreciate this. Wines will be assembled as "whites" or "Chablis type" or "Rhine type." The trouble is simply this: even as distinctive a description as a "Rhine type" is vague. There are several ways of making a "Rhine" that resembles the wines made on the Rhine. Furthermore, there are several ways of making a *varietal.* A varietal is simply a wine made from a specific grape (that grape must constitute at least 51 percent of the final wine—75 percent as of 1983). Many wineries make a varietal wine from virtually 100 percent of the variety of grape of the same name. Good examples are Fetzer, Beaulieu, and Robert Mondavi—three names of importance from the Napa-Mendocino-Sonoma Valley. But when a winery chooses to slip in at the 51 percent standard, barely, it's obvious that a varietal, until the new rules take effect in 1983, won't mean much. In the meantime, you'll have to rely on the reputation of the winery or on the occasional practice of noting the approximate varietal percentages on the label.

A good example of the misleading definitions on wine labels is the history of the Chenin Blanc varietal in California. The Charles Krug Winery pioneered the development of this grape in the fifties, finishing it with a fruity, quite sweet body. For years it was the only Chenin Blanc in general distribution, and so a generation of wine drinkers grew up with the idea that this must be what a Chenin Blanc grape tastes like. When, in the late sixties and seventies, dozens of other Chenin Blancs began to appear, the Krug "style" was so well accepted that lighter, drier versions were thought to be unauthentic. The premier wineries in California felt the need to label their versions "dry" or "semi-sweet" to warn unsuspecting customers. This particular grape (along with many other varieties) grows quite differently in the various climatic regions of the state, compounding the confusion. Nowadays it is heavily planted in secondary locations and has become one of the "everyday" varietals well suited to jugs.

A similar thing happened to the Green Hungarian popularized by the Buena Vista Winery about the same time. It, too, was fruity and sweet enough to attract the newcomer to wine drinking. In fact, there was perhaps 40 percent Chenin Blanc in it. When Weibel brought out its version many years later, many connoisseurs thought it was not up to the Buena Vista standard. But Weibel has made it into a very popular jug type, in a classic magnum bottle. Its dry style is now the "standard."

As the public taste can change rapidly, so can any individual's. Over the past two decades, sweet dessert wines have fallen into relative disfavor. And if the public continues to behave like most individuals, it will move from the current fascination with white wines to the drier reds that fully test the palate. Thus a typical evolution of taste in a wine drinker might be from cooking sherry to Harvey's Bristol Cream, to a fruity Rhine, on to a California Chablis, a rosé, a bubbly Lambrusco, to a jug red, and finally a red varietal. The "pop wine" craze of the sixties turned out to be a dead end in this maze, and it demonstrated once and for all that the taste in one's mouth can very well be evidence of bad taste.

Good taste, and educated taste, comes only after many tastes-in-the-mouth. The trial and error process can be shortened, however, by relying somewhat on the judgment of others. If you're drinking a sweet table wine because it's something you've always liked, perhaps it's time to test the waters of dry wines and red wines. It's difficult to break away from established food habits—from oversalting your food or oversugaring your cereal. Sugar in wine, in fact, is objectionable not as a taste in itself (it is of the essence of the French Sauternes) but because it tends to mask other flavors as it masks them in food. Unfortunately, one of the more difficult things in life is to pass on to someone else your sensation of taste.

THE WINE TASTING PROBLEM

Many wine tastings are, of course, only polite excuses to have a party. The other kind, at which wines are seriously evaluated either for the awarding of prizes or the ranking of wines in a newsletter, has problems all its own. Standards are necessarily vague, and language hasn't kept pace with our sensations. Thus the *Wine Steward* newsletter (see Appendix) says that a '71 Schloss Vollrad Spätlese "musically goes well with Bach's 2nd Piano Concerto," and that a '62 Cheval Blanc has "the aftertaste of silence." Wine makers have similar problems trying to label their products. They know that many consumers secretly like wines slightly sweeter than they would ever admit, so they say "semisweet" when the product is actually quite high in sugar, and they say "dry" when it's semisweet.

The very naming of wine types is fraught with paradoxes—and, like the word "jug," is historically conditioned. The three most common names for jug wines—Chablis, Rhine, and Burgundy—are the unhappy result of the historical accident that French and German wines were the models of the industry when Californians entered the wine scene in the middle of the nineteenth century. These names do serve a modest purpose: they tell us if the wine is white or red and supposedly whether it's sweet (Rhine) or dry (Chablis) or "hearty" (Burgundy). One would think that the color of the wine would be obvious, yet many wineries put out a "Chablis Blanc." The label designation "Sauterne" has now fallen from favor, yet when it is used it never, to my knowledge, accurately names anything like the great product of Sauternes—a dessert wine. There are two great red wine regions in France, Bordeaux and Burgundy, so one would logically expect some sort of jug name to describe a Bordeaux type. Many "Clarets" are now appearing, as yet with no consistent distinction from "Burgundies."

The first stage in the education of one's taste is to learn the difference between names that mean something and those that do not. All right: at least "Rhine" means that the wine should be fruitier and usually sweeter. Many of the progressive California makers are now dropping "Burgundy" in favor of, simply, "Red Table Wine." I would think that we can safely keep these *generic* names as long as no one labors under the delusion that there's a Chablis *grape* (the main grape of the region is Pinot Chardonnay, and there's not much of that). And the generic names may be useful when restaurants and bars begin offering *two* house whites, a Chablis type and a Rhine type. Next one should learn the major grape varieties: Cabernet Sauvignon, Zinfandel, Pinot Noir, Petite Sirah, Carignane, and Gamay (among the reds), and Pinot Chardonnay, Gewürztraminer, Riesling, Sauvignon Blanc, Chenin Blanc, French Colombard, Green Hungarian, etc. (among the whites). The rosés shouldn't be overlooked, of course; and one should discriminate between a rosé made with the Grenache grape or similar and those made literally by mixing reds and whites. A relatively new type, not likely to appear in jugs for some time, is the light grape (either rosé or dusky in color) made from black (red) grapes fermented off their skins. These wines are the result of the overabundance of black grapes in recent years, and have given us a new category of designations to wrestle with: Cabernet Blanc, Nectar of Zinfandel, and all kinds of "rosé" combinations.

As we will see in chapter 6, one of the best ways to straighten things out in your mind when it comes to wine is *to learn how to make it*. This is not as imposing a task as it may seem; a quick tour of a winery is often enough, or a perusal of a few issues of a good newsletter. If you now have, at least, the names on the labels fixed in a scale of values, you can now tackle the thornier problem of how to read a wine-tasting result.

The problem of wine tastings conducted to rank wines in order of preference is simply that *preference for what* is seldom stated. Some wines are meant for quaffing, some for sipping, others for washing dinner down, others for enhancing the flavors of foods. There's an old French axiom, "Buy wines with apples, sell them with cheese": apples put wine to the acid test (quite literally), while cheese shows them off. Should a wine be criticized for being "thin"? Thin wines are usually the best quaffing wines. While it may be said that sweetness rarely helps a red wine, sweetness can enchance a white—which is why among the nonfortified wines the only dessert wines are white. Why should the suggestion of green peppers be desirable in a cabernet, as wine buffs claim, when it's disastrous in a Riesling?

So we have two immediate problems in any wine tasting before the first sip is taken: the range of styles is enormous, and the intended uses of wines are seldom taken into account. And yet we confidently rank wines one, two, three, etc., as if it were the order of the finish in a race.

In attempting to make sense out of the wide variety of jug wines currently available, I conducted numerous wine tastings in four major cities: San Francisco, Los Angeles, Chicago, and New York. I also duly noted the wine tastings conducted for newspaper polls, magazine articles, and wine societies. In the end it became obvious that the usual one-two-three ranking method simply didn't take into account (1) the style of the wine maker, (2) the intended use of the wine, and (3) the taste preference of the drinker. Wine critics tend to emphasize dryness because the ultimate in their chosen profession is the appreciation of those small nuances in flavor, obvious in the great wines, which would be overwhelmed by even minimal sweetness. Jug wines, in general, allow the wine maker greater latitude in settling on a style for a given wine, and, strangely enough, have a wider variety of uses than premium wines. No one with any sense uncorks a Beaulieu Private Reserve to sip while puttering around the garden. Finally, jug wines have the potential of remaining pretty much the same from year to year—because they can be blended from various years and various grapes. For all of these reasons, a new way of judging jug wines presents itself, which I call the "benchmark" method.

BENCHMARK WINES: ISLANDS OF TRUTH

Wines are commonly judged by three systems, from sophisticated to just plain sloppy. The Enology Department of the University of California at Davis, without doubt the premier wine institution in the world, devised a point system that is most commonly used in serious tastings. Points are awarded in various categories, such as aroma, color, balance, sweetness, finish: twenty points is tops. With a dozen or more wines under scrutiny, the values generally range from nine to fourteen—even in the case of premium wines. The very comprehensiveness of this scale makes it inappropriate for jug wines. With few exceptions, no attempt is made to breed noticeable aromas into them, their colors are predictable and clean, and few have benefited from aging, in or out of oak.

For all of these reasons, jug wines are typically criticized in twenty-point judgings as being boring or uninteresting. With the advent of varietals like Cabernet and French Colombard in jugs, this is changing. Nevertheless, for a long time to come the vast majority of jugs will be the generics—for which the standards of premium wines are meaningless. The person who buys a sports car for pleasure driving wants it to be "interesting"; the person who buys a workhorse car for transportation wants it to be so boring as to never surprise him.

A less formal system, devised by Fred Cherry, publisher of *Bottles Up*, makes more sense with jug wines and is also a surprisingly simple way to judge premium wines, too. I suspect that his system has been used unconsciously by most wine enthusiasts in their private tastings. Fred's idea is that a wine is innocent until proven guilty—and so should be accorded a full ten points at the start. Then deductions can be made, up to two points each, for defects that strike the eye, the nose, and the throat. Sight, smell, and taste are, after all, the only measures we have. Finally, the entire impression of the wine is worth four points to start with, and deductions on any grounds not covered by eye, nose, and throat are allowed up to that figure. The result is usually higher figures, up to a maximum of ten, of course. In the case of jug wines, however, the same objection applies as to the twenty-point system: the eye and the nose seldom have anything to tell us.

Finally, there's the plain old "I like it" judging system. Each taster simply rates the wines one, two, three, etc., and the scores of all tasters are compiled. As in golf, the lowest total is the best. I have seen this system used to rank jug wines with the rationale that simple wines deserve a simple rating system. Yet the opposite is closer to the truth. Since jug wines differ mainly in style rather than in discernible qualities, an "I like it" system is really only a poll of the preferences of the tasters. And sometimes the preferences are prejudiced by the laziness of the organizers of the tasting in disguising the bottles properly. In one tasting I witnessed for a San Francisco newspaper, bottles were "brown-bagged" to preserve their anonymity. This works fine for fifths, but it was obvious to the tasters that the tall, slim magnum shapes of some of the bottles and the lack of threads for a screw cap indicated that these were costlier brands.

In the benchmark system, there really isn't any need to disguise the bottles. The idea is to select one wine well known to all the tasters. To be a benchmark it must be readily available, fairly consistent from year to year, and of medium to high quality. It is a little island of truth from which piers can be sent out into the sea of uncertainty. What the tasters do is to compare the other wines in the selection with this benchmark—not better or worse, but sweeter or drier, lighter or fuller, fruitier or flatter. There is no limit on the number of categories to be compared, but these are surely the most common. If the tasting is conducted at a restaurant, as many of mine were, the house wine usually makes a good benchmark. The benchmark wines I've selected for this book are the result of those tastings and my own experience with the progress of various well-known wines over the years.

Please don't take benchmark status as a recommendation, for better or worse. These wines I've chosen for this purpose are simply available throughout the country, will probably always taste just about the same as they do now, and have no obvious defects.

The result of a benchmark tasting is not a ranking, but a factual description. For example, Paul Masson Emerald Dry is not as sweet, but fruitier and more complex, than the benchmark Alamadén Mountain Rhine. This description may tell you that you would probably prefer one to the other; it would tell someone else the opposite. Or it may tell you that you would prefer one to the other with a certain kind of meal. There is, after all, a great deal of objectivity possible even in an area as personal as this. You may like red wines with fish, but your taste buds are out of step with those of most of the rest of us. The acids in a good, dry white wine tend to balance the oils in seafood; a good rosé seems to go well with ham, for some reason—the same reason, perhaps, that it takes a big red to match the food values in a steak. This, too, is part of educating one's taste.

According to your own preferences in food and drinking occasions, you can rank wines in one, two, three fashion—but these will be merely your personal preferences. The great advantage of this system is that it also guides the development of your taste along the known standards of sweet, bitter, acid, and salt. Clever though he may be, no wine maker can tamper with these registers of taste. If you want to test a wine for sweetness (and not confuse it with fruitiness--a common mistake), you can dip just the point of your tongue into a full glass of wine. Since only the sensation of sweetness is felt there, your palate will not be confused by the other three basic tastes.

The appreciation of jug wines is an economical way to prepare yourself for more adventurous explorations of the fruit of the vine. In a sense, we are far better off than our counterparts before Prohibition. Their wines were certainly honest and cheap, but the everyday wines of today are consistent as well. Consistency, in fact, is the danger of jug wines as well as their greatest asset. Striving to please the greatest number of customers and to offend no one, will the jug wine producers gradually drift toward the same innocuous product? Experience has shown the contrary. There are about three hundred producing wineries in California alone, and even the smallest are turning to some sort of "everyday wine."

In the description of wines on the following pages, I've purposely concentrated on California producers. Italian and French "jugs"—really the magnum sizes for the most part—are a big factor in the two major wine markets of New York and Washington, D.C., and will continue to grow in importance elsewhere. But they are so different in background and so inconsistent in quality that they generally fail to qualify, as we will see, for the definition of jug wines I propose to use. In volume, Italian wines now account for about half the U.S. imports and in time will challenge their California counterparts for quality as well as price.

Many English as well as American wine writers have confirmed the general impression that the everyday wines of America are quite superior to the *vin ordinaire* of the Mediterranean countries. This would have been heresy ten years ago. Have the American wines improved that much? Charles Crawford, the genial enologist at Gallo since 1942, told me that he believes the jug wines of today are generally better than the premium wines of California 25 years ago. That's a strong statement, and memory is a treacherous thing; but enologists from equally prestigious wineries, who were tasting their own products quite carefully 25 years ago, confirmed this judgment.

Let's take a taste and see.

2

Everyday Wines

*We must teach our children that it is not the year, the
producer, or even the label that determines the quality
of the wine; it is the wine in the glass, whatever the
label or producer or year. It is a sin to allow a son (or
daughter) to grow up thinking that because the label
says Chateau Lafite-Rothschild 1963 and costs $30
that it is a fine wine. In this particular case, it is a poor
wine. Drink wine, not labels.*

> —Dr. Maynard Amerine, *Professor Emeritus of
> Enology, University of California at Davis*

The wine makers with whom I've talked confirm unanimously that the
best word for what we've heretofore called "jug" wines is "everyday"
wines. Yet it seems to me this is too self-serving a designation to stick.
Let's upgrade the wine in the jug and let the words fall where they may.
Nevertheless, "everyday wines" is the best *concept* of what we're talking
about.

A wine that's drinkable every day has to have these things going for it:
(1) it must be affordable; (2) it must appeal to a wide variety of tastes; and
(3) it must be fairly consistent from year to year. In the past, I would have
added some physical dimensions: it must come in a container larger than a
fifth, with a screw top rather than cork "finish," as they say in the trade,
and with a generic name on the label instead of a varietal (Burgundy, not
Pinot Noir). How times have changed! Some of the best everyday wines
come in fifths, with corks, and are as much as 75 percent Chenin Blanc,
French Colombard, or Zinfandel. Under my three guidelines above, these
wines should really be thought of as jug wines. To echo Dr. Amerine, drink
wine—not screw caps, bottles, or generic names on labels!

THE TYRANNY OF THE FIFTH

It has taken a long time, but the fifth of a gallon is steadily losing its magic as a symbol of quality. Strictly speaking, it's no longer a fifth but 750 milliliters (three-quarters of a liter). These two sizes are nearly equal, so the conversion to the metric system should go smoothly for wine drinkers. As of January 1, 1979, gallons, half-gallons, and fifths were no longer shipped (if you find one on a shelf, it was purchased by the store before that date). The common denominator of jugs has become the 1.5 liter, roughly equivalent to two fifths or the magnum. In place of the gallon there's the 3 liter, which many producers started using in 1978 without changing the price from the gallon (a loss to the unwary buyer of just about a fifth of a gallon). A few of the more thoughtful wine makers, such as San Antonio (Los Angeles), have moved up to the 4-liter size— because their major market for the larger containers is the restaurant trade; and restaurateurs watch sizes very carefully.

Incidentally, you really have to remember only three things in making the conversion to metric: (1) what looks like a fifth contains just about the same amount; (2) what looks like a gallon is often a fifth *less;* and (3) in unusual containers, figure two and a half of these large containers for every two gallons.

The key to the dominance of the fifth has long been its association with corks—and the longer the cork the better. Two trends have finally broken this love affair: more and more vintners have been putting quality wines

The 1.5-liter shape has many variations from the traditional magnum, and words like "Claret" and "Napa" are beginning to appear on them.

under screw caps, and more and more have been using corks in the larger size bottles.

Almadén pioneered the use of cork-type closures on its Mountain line of jugs in the tear-shaped bottles. It was a neat transition: after the plastic seal was removed, the cork could be removed simply by twisting a knob attached to its top. This convenient stopper, borrowed from ports and sherries, lent an aura of quality to the image created by the pleasant green bottles and well-designed labels.

More recently, Robert Mondavi and Fetzer have introduced corks in traditional magnum sizes of generic wines. And, in the other direction, Gallo has taken to corks for its premium fifths, under the Ernest and Julio label. As we will see in chapter 6, there is no clear-cut answer to the question of whether corks are better, worth the extra cost, or just a pretense for the dinner table.

By far the strongest influence against a slavish adherence to corks has been Gallo. Even after their Chablis Blanc and Hearty Burgundy became accepted in fine restaurants as a result of sensational national publicity, wine stewards didn't know quite how to handle them. I recall an amusing scene at Shepherd's in the Drake Hotel, in New York City, when one of our party put in a request for a California white. The steward confessed that he had none except Gallo Chablis Blanc, which had just been the subject of a glowing account in *Consumer Reports*. It was brought to the table and shown to our host. The price was still visible in a corner of the label: $1.79. Our host nodded his acceptance, and the steward promptly sunk his corkscrew into the metal cap.

What most people fail to remember about the Gallo line is that it was the same wine no matter what the container—and still is, with the exception of the newer labels. Gallo's chief enologist told me that this was the result of the preferences of their early customers—largely Italian families in the metropolitan centers of the East. They were fiercely loyal and expected the same wine under the same label—the "Pastoso et Scelto," from which the more recent name "Hearty Burgundy" was derived. Over the years Gallo paid the price for its stubbornness: it earned the reputation for having "jug quality" in everything it did. But who has the last laugh now?

That the fifth no longer has special magic with consumers is evidenced by such fine wineries as Christian Brothers and Charles Krug bottling the same wine in 1.5 liters as in 750 milliliters. Neither the container nor the cork nor the label really defines the difference between jugs and premium wines.

AFFORDABLE, CONSISTENT, WIDELY APPEALING

In these inflationary times, one must be careful to talk about what is or isn't affordable. One must also remember that the major California jug wines can cost as much as 50 percent more in the East than in their home state. And that's in normal times. The lifting of the fair trade laws in California spawned the opening of discount wine and liquor stores which shaved prices to the wholesale level. After paying, in San Francisco, about three dollars for a 1.5 liter of Robert Mondavi Red Table Wine, I was appalled to see it selling at nearly twice as much in New York City.

Three of the great names of the Napa Valley. Some are now producing jug wines (Christian Brothers); others under a secondary label (Beringer's Los Hermanos); and others, perhaps, never will (Beaulieu and Charles Krug).

In general, however, it's fair to say that a bottle costing more than six dollars in the magnum or 1.5-liter size can scarcely be considered an everyday wine. What does one do when a 3-liter bottle is offered for about $2.70—quite common in California—and a slightly better wine is twice as much? Which is the jug? Is it a matter of relativity? I have attempted to overcome this problem by dividing jugs into three categories based simply on *varying degrees of affordability*. The middle range is deserving, I think, of the appellation "everyday wines." These will be judged in this chapter. At the two extremes of price, but still in this range, I will rank "Jugs Ordinaire" and "A Sunday Kind of Jug" in following chapters. Any number of other classifications could have been made, but it's my experience that this breakdown on the basis of cost, pure and simple, is an important factor with most wine buyers.

The other two factors, consistency and wide appeal, are of course more subjective. Yet it's evident that wines made from Eastern varieties such as

Concord or Catawba aren't favored as table wines or quaffing wines by any but the most provincial. Similarly, this standard rules out many imports, such as the cheaper German Rhines or Moselles with an alcoholic content around 9 percent, or the French and Italian *vin ordinaire* that are just too harsh for American sensibilities. A lack of consistency from year to year would tend to disqualify many of the smaller New York and California wineries. One of the pleasures of wine appreciation is that search for the great discovery—the inexpensive jug that outclasses a ten-dollar bottle, the Burgundy that turns out to be 100 percent Pinot Noir, the Chablis that somehow sports an oak nose. All right; but these cannot be considered everyday wines—unless you were able to corner the market on your rare find. (Occasionally this happens; before Sutter Home came into prominence as one of the finer small Napa Valley wineries, a friend of mine snapped up forty cases of their Burgundy that he discovered had been aged in oak for several years and consisted completely of Carignane and Pinot Noir.)

The rules, as I have set them up, thus favor the California jug wines. This is not to say the others are disapproved of—only that consideration of them as everyday wines would be meaningless. I hope that this will not be considered blatant chauvinism on my part; if you had searched the liquor stores as I have over the past year I think you would come to the same conclusion.

I have mentioned that consistency and wide appeal are not unmitigated blessings; others might prefer to avoid jugs altogether just because they are common, bland, ordinary. French wine makers generally find the California whites to be insipid or cloying. New York's Governor Hugh Carey has been a conspicuous supporter of the local product. In a letter to Walter Taylor, owner of Bully Hill Vineyards, he capped his praise of New York vintners with this handwritten postscript, reproduced in the company's quarterly newsletter: "My anti-Almadén crusade is taking root—the Californians are the barbarians of the vineyards."

DRY WINE ELITISM

A tour of a Napa Valley winery has just been completed. The guide leads the group of tourists to the tasting room for the final ritual. He asks, "What would you like to try among the whites?" Most answer, "Something dry." Their first taste elicits "Oos" and "Ahs." They continue on through sweeter wines, then the reds, and finally a sweet white dessert wine like Malvasia Bianca or Muscato Amabile. On the way out most of them buy the dessert wine or one of the sweeter white table wines. What happened to their preference for something dry?

The large wineries have universally noticed that the word "dry" has become a catchword, possibly originating in the "dry martini" or in the tendency of wine writers to extol dryness but seldom sweetness. In any event, a research program conducted in 1977 by Mogen David Wine

California
WHITE TABLE WINE
ALCOHOL 12% BY VOLUME
PREPARED AND BOTTLED BY
'ROBERT MONDAVI WINERY
OAKVILLE, NAPA VALLEY, CALIFORNIA

A wine for everyday use made entirely of varietal wine grapes. Flavorful and complex in character.

More and more, labels are becoming informative: though often couched in flowery terms, the descriptions are as accurate as one could hope for in such a subjective matter as taste. When it comes to sweetness, for instance, one Gallo wine has a "whisper," Paul Masson a "mysterious trace," and Almadén is "slightly."

Corporation turned up the finding that 70 percent of the wine-drinking population in America actually prefer sweet to dry wines. The company's marketing director says, "Our target is pure middle America. We're after people who drink Coke, eat hot dogs, and drive Chevrolets."

There are other indications that the preference for sweetness by "middle America" is indeed a factor in introducing new wines to the public—but perhaps not in holding their interest. At the height of the pop wine craze, it was virtually impossible to buy frozen raspberries in grocery stores: they were all going into the production of berry wines. Now the raspberries are back. Similarly, a pragmatic Italian surveyed American popular taste a few years back and decided to create a wine just for that taste: thus was born Lambrusco. In its home territory this wine is nothing like the fizzy, sugary product we are blessed with. But my experience is that wine drinkers move through this soda pop stage rather quickly. They may still prefer a little sweetness in their whites, but not Coca Cola syrup.

If there is a "dry wine elitism," as Mogen David asserts, it shows itself in critics of jug wines who dismiss sweetness as inherently damaging to a table wine. As I have mentioned in chapter 1, this criticism does everyday wines the injustice of ignoring where they are usually drunk: not at the table, but in the armchair and on the patio.

Sweetness may have much to do, in fact, with one characteristic that will be mentioned often in the following comparisons: body. Body is easy to picture but hard to define. Lack of body is thinness, wateryness; excess body is a fullness that overwhelms other aspects of the wine, a hot, volatile sensation. A combination of fruit, sugar, and acids is what gives a wine body—after all, the only thing left in wine is alcohol, water, and minerals.

It may help to compare other drinks to see what is meant by the four tastes of acid, sweet, bitter, and salt. Tomato juice or lemon juice produces the sensation of acidity. Orange juice is usually overwhelmingly sweet. Bitterness is sensed in grapefruit juice and beer. Although we all know what salt tastes like, in a drink it is usually quite subtle; bouillon would be a gross example, tea perhaps a closer one.

A few other comparisons are in order as a preliminary to the following "tasting." The sense of smell is all-important to taste; with one's eyes and nose shut, an onion tastes surprisingly like an apple. Yet wine writers usually refer to smell as distinct from taste (and they use that pretentious and seldom necessary word, "nose," to boot). "Nose" applies both to aroma (the characteristic smell of the grape) and to bouquet (the smells originating from the vintner's art—fermenting, aging, refining). In tasting it helps to sniff the wine fully before sipping, because these smells are so evanescent. They are also rare in jugs. If you've ever tasted a good bourbon, you proably know what oak smells like; better, you can seek out a French or Yugoslavian oak barrel at a winery and sniff it. (As we will see in chapter 6, not everyone agrees that barrel-aging is always good; as John Parducci put it, "How could critics compare, vintners discuss, wine lovers appreciate the true varietal character of aged Cabernet when we had never experienced the wine not altered by wood contact?") Smoothness is the result of a pleasant balance of tastes, with none predominating. Finally, "finish" is the lingering aftertaste of the wine, perhaps a product of body and smoothness.

In the following comparisons, I will take time out here and there to mention in more detail some specific sensations of the palate.

Everyday Wines: Chablis Type

"I'll have a glass of Chablis—California Chablis,"
he tells the waiter. "That's all I drink now. Jug
wine. California jug wine."
—Erskine Caldwell, at 75, interviewed
in *The San Francisco Chronicle*

The Standards: According to the California Wine Institute Technical Committee, "California Chablis" should be, in color, light-to-medium straw-yellow. Its body should be light to medium, with medium acidity and fruit. The committee adds that the wine should be well balanced, but this is just as vague a description as the supposedly objective criteria mentioned above. In reality, any wine maker can call any white wine a Chablis, but almost all reserve this term for the drier, thinner whites. No grape varieties are mentioned; it is assumed that Thompson Seedless, the most abundant and really not a wine grape, will find its way into most "Chablis." The word "Mountain" on the label is a backhanded way of implying that other grapes account for the bulk of the wine—since Thompson Seedless is grown almost exclusively in the Sacramento-San Joaquin Valley and other regions with the same climatic features. (See Appendix for California wine regions.)

The irony of the Chablis designation is that almost certainly no Pinot Chardonnay—the most expensive grape grown in this country—goes into California Chablis—yet it is the grape of the Chablis region of France. In reading wine columnists and critics one should be careful about references to Chablis. Writers with European orientations tend to mean Chablis quite literally—and so they might advise one to invest in a Chablis "first growth." Only a handful of wine merchants—and these in New York and Washington, D.C.—mark their bins so precisely that one could easily find a first-growth Chablis by walking into the store. American wine enthusiasts, on the other hand, usually mean California Chablis when they ask for a Chablis, and rarely add "California."

The Benchmark: C. K. Mondavi Chablis. I should emphasize again that the benchmark wine is not necessarily the best of the lot, in my opinion or in anybody else's. It is simply a known quantity, with fairly obvious characteristics. Inevitably, however, some readers will want to try the benchmark wines first (of course it's not necessary). So I've also tried to be as objective as possible by not choosing a benchmark from any winery where I am known or have friends.

In terms of 1.5 liters, or magnums, all the benchmark wines range in price between three and four dollars (slightly higher east of the Mississippi!). Prices on the other wines will not be mentioned unless they vary considerably from this standard.

**CALIFORNIA SELECT
CHABLIS**

MADE AND BOTTLED BY
C. Mondavi & Sons
ST. HELENA·CALIFORNIA
ALCOHOL 12% BY VOLUME

CALIFORNIA SELECT
CHABLIS

CK Mondavi Select Chablis resembles in general character the Chablis (White Burgundy) imported from Europe. This Chablis is a select California wine with a more delicate bouquet than Dry Sauterne. This ever popular dry white wine is crisp, well balanced and dependable, and is a Blue Point's best friend. Serve it well chilled with fish, shellfish, chicken and light foods in general.

C. Mondavi & Sons

Now—what is the Mondavi Chablis like? The makers have added the word "Select" to the name, and call it "dependable" on the back label. I would agree. Though mild overall, it's not insipid: sugar, fruit, color, and acidity are all there. Some tasters sense a slight bouquet. Its aftertaste may be too astringent for some. It consistently scores in the upper middle in the tastings I've seen and conducted.

HIGHER-PRICED CHABLIS

In the four to five dollar range for 1.5 liters are several nationally available generics and a few in limited distribution—in a wide range of styles. The elder statesman is Paul Masson's Emerald Dry White Table

Wine, which has earned the respect of European visitors for many years. Its burst of fruit flavors is immediately appealing, and the roundness doesn't turn to a cloying sweetness in the aftertaste. Quite a bit sweeter than the Mondavi, it has also the body to carry it—and enough to match spicy foods as well as richer fish and fowl. It is accordingly a favorite in many Chinese restaurants. Emerald, by the way, is a grape hybrid introduced by Masson and not widely available—in a class with the Charbono from Inglenook. (When you hear a wine critic advising you to try some Emerald Dry or Charbono, you can guess that he is steering you to a friendly winery without letting on.) This classy wine is a good example of a well-respected fifth going to the larger size to save you the price of the extra glass.

Less golden in color and fruitiness is Christian Brothers Select Chablis—not widely available in Eastern markets. One might guess that the similarity to Mondavi's Chablis is no accident; they are neighbors, even if much of the grape is brought from the Valley. If anything, the Christian Brothers version is a little weaker all around, except in the attempt at bouquet and a touch more sweetness.

Sonoma Vineyards has gone through many vicissitudes in its short history, but now seems to have settled into serious wine making. Not really an important name among Californians, it compounded its anonymity several years ago by attempting to merchandise wine by mail, with gimmicks such as personalized labels and gift boxes. It has achieved consistency by concentrating on varietals, its Northern California French Colombard and Chenin Blanc, both with vintage dates, surprising the experts. The varietals themselves don't prove anything: there are few other cheaper whites available in its locale to assemble for a Chablis. Compared to our benchmark, Mondavi, you can expect more adventure here—more acid, more tartness, about the same color and sweetness in the background, with the Chenin Blanc somewhat fruitier. Again, Sonoma Vineyards isn't yet a household word beyond the state lines.

Quite widely known is Inglenook—but you have to watch details on the label. In the price range we're discussing, their North Coast Counties Vintage Chablis is at the low side of the scale, but in other respects is a contender for honors. Its main difference from the Mondavi is its attempt at dryness, still retaining enough fruitiness to be interesting. In color and body it tends to lightness, but preserves a delicacy not always there in the Navalle line from the same maker.

The other attempts at a truly dry, European-style Chablis have come from three premium wineries. I suspect their efforts have been misunderstood, because they show up all over the lot in wine tastings. They seem to be aiming more at another well-known French type—the Loire wines of Muscadet and Sancerre. After all, few if any of the grapes used

for these jugs is Chardonnay and most are Chenin Blanc, the grape of the
Loire region. Alas, there is no duplicating the way that grape grows in the
chalky, moist valleys west of Paris. Hemingway reputedly leaned to Sancerre, but Peter Buckley tells me the author leaned to whatever was most
available. What is certain is there is no bite quite like the Loire Valley
wines, high or low brow. Robert Mondavi has taken great risks to capture
this flinty dryness, and so his White Table Wine, at the high end of the
price range we're considering, often seems to our tastes to be off in
bouquet and aftertaste. As we will see in chapter 6, Robert's winery is one
of the models of modern design and efficiency; he set out deliberately to
make his own name in the field after a divisive family struggle for the
inheritance of the Krug estate. Things have been patched up now, but it
must please the C. K. winery to come ahead of Robert in tastings. The
bottom line: compared to our benchmark, the White Table Wine of
Robert Mondavi has everything but the sweetness, and so seems "green"
by comparision with C. K.'s mellowness.

At the same exalted price level, the Fetzer attempt at a Premium
White is more conventional though equally dry and fruity. There's no
lingering bite here, but nothing dramatic, either. It achieves a little more
flavor than the Mondavi Chablis but is essentially different in its pronounced dryness.

At the head of the Napa Valley of the Mondavis, the Inglenooks, and
the Christian Brothers stands a Mediterranean-style cluster of white-stuc-
coed buildings on a proud plateau. Reached by visitors only on a Disneyland type of gondola, this is the home of Sterling Vineyards. As we will see
in chapter 6, it is the wine tourer's delight, and, when Sterling began to
make an everyday wine some years ago, it signalled a new phase in the jug
wine boom. The newest of the larger wineries, Sterling was able to put
great quantities of wine into new oak barrels. There is perhaps more oak,
as a result, in their White Table Wine than in any other jug at any cost.
There is certainly a lot of style: full of color yet crisp, sweetness completely under control, mellowness in the finish. Once the Sterling line was
available only at the winery and selected restaurants; it's now offered by
mail and in major stores, but seldom in the East. Against Mondavi Chablis
one would have to say that it's simply a more complete wine, tending to
dryness. In this case and that of Robert Mondavi and Fetzer, comparisons
are invidious because these seem to be made specifically for the table—not
for sipping with ice cubes or chilled as an aperitif.

MEDIUM-PRICED CHABLIS

Inglenook's Navalle Chablis is often seen on airlines and in popular restaurants—a good gauge of its inoffensiveness. When the venerable St. Helena winery was sold to Nestlé, connoisseurs despaired of ever seeing a fine Inglenook again. Aggressive promotion and an overwrought advertising program aimed at making it a product for the masses confirmed this impression. Some wine merchants began putting the Inglenook line on the shelves with the jugs, instead of in the racks and bins. Nestlé, nevertheless, did win the war, boosting sales several hundred percent in a short time. Happily, they have also won back some of their followers. The Navalle line of generics is showing up well in major tastings and by 1979, on its one hundredth birthday, there was promise that Inglenook was on the way to another level of greatness. Its Chablis is best described, vis-à-vis Mondavi's, as richer: greater body in the mouth and a longer aftertaste, in spite of its clean, light impression in the glass.

Sebastiani's Mountain Chablis seems also upwardly mobile, in the best sense. Sebastiani was a sleeper for many years among its better-known neighbors in Napa Valley and Sonoma. In recent years the winery has shown an energy characteristic of its wines. The Chablis is bigger than the Mondavi benchmark, more astringent, and, if my taste is any judge, more variable from batch to batch; also to my taste is the attempt to reduce sweetness without losing balance. Its golden color is in sharp contrast, as is Mondavi's, to the well-known Gallo Chablis Blanc.

The main difficulty in fixing the taste of this worthy favorite is that Gallo offers several whites very close to it in characteristics and price. Their Sauterne is equally clean, with a touch of sweetness equal to our benchmark. The varietals Sauvignon Blanc and Chenin Blanc are exceptional values at just a little more per 1.5 liters and add a distinct grapiness to the aftertaste. All of them have a little more body, in spite of their whiteness in the glass. The differences are small, and they don't always add up in a wine tasting; most tasters have to swirl the few sips they take in their mouths and then spit them out, or else be overwhelmed by flavors, not to mention alcohol, before all the wines are sampled. As a result, the staying power or drinkability of a wine is seldom measured in a tasting. This is where the Gallo brothers' close attention to detail pays off. Their wines are definitely not bland, yet they can be sipped throughout a long meal or an afternoon without cloying. The silkiness and cleanness of semi-dry wines may seem unimpressive at first sip, but as presented by Gallo these qualities easily grow on one.

The color of Italian Swiss Colony's Colony Chablis is, on the other hand, a tip-off to a thinner, drier wine than either Gallo or Mondavi. But if dryness is what you're after, here it is in a most delicate presentation. The younger brother of Paul Masson's Emerald Dry is his Chablis, another pale wine like Colony. Yet the Paul Masson is fairly complex in character. What difference does color make, you might well ask, if it's no indication of the taste of the wine? Is it merely for appearance on the table? The contrast between the Colony and the Paul Masson Chablis answers this question to some extent. The rich color of the Sebastiani or the Emerald Dry is lacking in both Colony and Paul Masson Chablis, and so is acidity and fruit; but the Paul Masson benefits from the difference in grapes in its more southerly clime. The vintners have retained those characteristics of the grapes in the Paul Masson without trying to gain character from sugar. The Colony Chablis has a touch of sweetness, but not enough acidity or fruit to affect its color.

The Paul Masson Chablis, by the way, scored first among fifteen domestic jug wines in a professional tasting conducted in 1979 by *The Washington Post*; Fetzer Premium White and Inglenook Navalle Chablis were close seconds in a tie. All three received comments on their balance, roundness, or lack of defects. These are the characteristics that seem to win in blind tastings rather than positive statements, even though all three wines do have their distinctive qualities.

A better-publicized tasting became the subject of legal action by the Bureau of Alcohol, Tobacco, and Firearms in 1978 when the Taylor Wine Company defied an old ruling of the bureau against comparative claims of taste in advertising. A subsidiary of the Coca-Cola Company, Taylor was a newcomer to the California wine scene through its purchase of Monterey Vineyards. What better way to make a splash against its well-entrenched competitors than to name them in television commercials—after Taylor had routed them in wine tastings? Inglenook, Almadén, Sebastiani, and Mondavi were selected as the competition; the wines to be compared were the everyday generics: Rhine, Burgundy, Rosé, and Chablis. Twenty-seven professional tasters did, indeed, find Taylor "best" in the first three categories and second in the Chablis. When the TV commercials appeared, the uproar in wine circles was just what Taylor had hoped for. The president of Sterling, another Coca-Cola company, felt obliged to make his apologies in his company's newsletter. Other jug wine producers felt slighted by not being included in the select group of Taylor's competition. In the end it was a stalemate, Taylor having made its point and the Treasury Department not quite sure of its legal precedents for stopping the ads.

A notable omission from the competitors was, of course, Gallo. Partly to satisfy his curiosity and partly to set things right, Robert Lawrence Balzer, the pre-eminent wine critic in California, conducted a tasting of his own and published the results in his column in *The Los Angeles Times*. Taylor was matched against Inglenook, Almadén, Sebastiani, C. K. Mondavi, Gallo, and three others—not all vintners in each category of Chablis, Rhine, Rosé, and Burgundy. Balzer made no mention of the Taylor contretemps, but the timing was such that his readers, at any rate, saw the connection. The surprising result was not that Taylor failed to match its performance in its televised tasting, but that in such a subjective undertaking Taylor was consistently at or near the top! Easily first among the Rosés, Taylor Rhine was in a virtual tie for first, Taylor was a close second among the Burgundies, and in a virtual tie for second behind Gallo Chablis Blanc. Almadén was meanwhile shut out of the winner's circle in all four categories.

Taylor's California Cellars Chablis is an attractive white, similar in golden hue and fruitiness to Masson Emerald Dry. It's even sweeter than our benchmark, Mondavi, but is so big in other ways it drinks cleanly. The impress of Monterey County is plainly on it; if it weren't called a Chablis it might please those tasters who are accustomed to a thinner, less mouth-filling version.

Another old Northern California name that sold out to a conglomerate in the sixties is Beringer; fortunately, its everday wines were promulgated under the name Los Hermanos—after the brothers Beringer. Like the Navalle line, it had a rocky start. Now, without being distinctive, it's a fair equivalent in taste with C. K. Mondavi—perhaps a little lighter all around. The same can be said for Almadén's California Mountain White Chablis, long a staple as a house wine or airline selection. Against Mondavi, this Chablis offers more bouquet—the result of grapes from a drier clime. Though thinner, it finishes with crispness and little lingering sweetness.

Other major wine producers in this price range are Weibel, Louis Martini, Franzia, Parducci, Cresta Blanca, Summit, Guasti, Winemasters, and Pedroncelli. The latter is the most different from our benchmark, with a pleasantly dry bite—an excellent choice with food. It's at the upper range of our medium price level and is not widely distributed, but worth looking for. Among the rest, only the Guasti is as short on flavor, but again this works to the advantage of a dinner wine. All are good values, worthy of sampling for some variety in your quaffing. Louis Martini and Pedroncelli are simply "White."

NAVALLE® CHENIN BLANC
OF CALIFORNIA

Vinted and Bottled by Inglenook Vineyards
San Francisco. Calif. BW 1589. Alc 12% by Vol.

Two additional types of Chablis should be noted before going on to the low-priced wines. First there are the growing number of varietals—chiefly Riesling, Chenin Blanc, and French Colombard—that issue from the wineries mentioned above in addition to their Chablis or white. The Chenin Blanc grape is just not good enough in California to stand on its own, and is easily swamped when it's only 51 percent of a blend. The vintner must do other things with it, as Charles Krug has demonstrated for years. Don't assume even a 100 percent Chenin Blanc is necessarily better than a Chablis or white with a mixture of Thompson Seedless. Then there are also all sorts of descriptive names that can also be subsumed under the name "Chablis." There are Sauterne Blancs, Gold Chablis, White Burgundies, sometimes from the same maker with only a slight variation in taste. If an unusual name or a varietal is shown on the label it is worth exploring if you have already been satisfied with the major line of the producer, usually a Chablis. It's folly to try to catalog these ephemeral products in a book.

Second, there are many smaller wineries (often just bottlers) whose products are available only in close proximity to their headquarters. An interesting example is the James Arthur Field Chablis. This very real gentleman selects batches of fermented grapes from various wineries in Northern California and has them finished to his specifications. This year it may be Healdsburg, next year San Jose. Mr. Field employs a simple but quite informative label and can be counted on to produce a refined, uncloying wine. A major liquor store chain in Northern California does pretty much the same thing on a larger scale: Ernie's. The subject of great excitement from a story in *The New York Times* several years back, this discount chain buys odd lots from small wineries, specializes in an enormous selection of the very best French and California fifths, and supplements these with varietals bottled under its own label. Then there are the small wineries that could easily expand, if they had the urge or the capital to do so, who produce a highly individual wine from year to year. Cambiaso California Chablis is bigger and more aromatic than most of the ones mentioned above; Barengo has a Chablis and a French Colombard of varying interest from year to year; and Valley of the Moon and d'Agostini have faithful customers among restaurants and retail outlets in their vicinity. It would serve no purpose to mention the dozens of other vintners or bottlers of dry white types—it's just nice to know they're there when you want to go exploring. (See chapter 6.)

This is a good time to mention that the array of designations on a California label come down to a few simple principles: (1) The winery on the label can be said to have "produced" the wine if it fermented at least 75 percent of it; and (2) All other words decribing the wine making process, such as "vinted by," "prepared by," "blended by," or "manufactured by" mean no more than that the winery bottled and labeled it. There is no restriction on the number of dba's (doing business as) a winery may employ; thus many large wineries operate one or more "wineries" under other names, either to gain more shelf space in stores or to market a product of lesser quality. When prestigious wineries such as Joseph Phelps in Napa Valley choose secondary labels, the result is often better than the first-line product of the nationally advertised brands! In jug wines, of course, the result is often, but not always, simply lower price.

LOW-PRICED CHABLIS

Without exception, the low-priced white wines generally available in jugs originate in the warmer, valley regions of California. At one time these valleys produced few of the true wine-grape varieties, and all had to be so heavily irrigated that the resulting fruit was light in flavor. This judgment survives today, even though better plantings, new hybrids developed at Davis, and concern for quality in vinification have made the interior valleys of the state quite hospitable to excellent wines. A few bold souls have even flung the challenge back at the wineries who insist on putting "Mountain" on their labels: they're now labeling themselves "Valley Chablis"!

Some of the wineries in this category are on the borderline between medium and low cost. Foppiano Chablis, at considerably under three dollars for 1.5 liters, is a flavorsome, uncloying wine; it took second place in a blind tasting of fifteen whites in San Francisco recently. But then Petri Chablis Blanc, a lighter version, well under two dollars for 1.5 liters, came in third! Guasti's French Colombard and the Guimarra Classic California Chablis are also in the top of the low-cost category—both from the southern part of the state and both establishing a reputation for their own labels after having produced wines for others for decades. Guasti is one of the family known as the California Wine Association, a trade name of the Perelli-Minetti Winery. Giumarra is another sleeping giant, whose quality is improving with its volume. The Chablis style here is earthier than further up the valley, lacking some of the flavor of our benchmark, Mondavi. The Chablis Blanc of Delicato and the Mountain Chablis of Famiglia Cribari are well under three dollars for 1.5 liters, thinner than the benchmark, but also nicely acidic. The latter brand was right up with the leaders in *The Washington Post* tasting mentioned earlier. On Growers, see the next section.

At roughly the same price level are two unusual wineries farther north, near the end of San Francisco Bay. San Martin was once simply a roadside tasting room with all sorts of fruit wines and ordinary varietals. It's now upgrading all along the line, and its most recent Chablis, labeled Mountain, is a complex blend quite unlike any of the styles already described. It certainly doesn't err on the side of sweetness, and the price makes it an affordable adventure. As it further emulates the finer wineries, however, it can be expected to move into the medium-priced category. The other surprise, and a recent one too, in this locale is Emile's. The Emilio Guglielmo family has been making wine there for more than half a century, but only in the last few years has it acquired the status of discovery. I prefer the drier Blanc Sec to the Chablis, yet in both instances the wine has staying power in its freedom from any cloying aspects. Their enologist says that they pride themselves on keeping their refining to a minimum and relying on proper grape selection for balance in the finished product. Only a winery of modest size can hope for this desideratum. Many of the best French bistros in the Bay Area use Emile's as a house wine—I don't know if there is any connection between this and the change from Emilio's to their present name!

Finally we come with a vengeance to everyday wines: the trio of Carlo Rossi, Yosemite Road, and JFJ Winery. The first may be a familiar name anywhere in the country, because it's Gallo's secondary line, and nobody, but nobody, distributes like Gallo. For more than five years now, nothing with the Gallo label has contained Thompson Seedless. These lesser grapes, if you can call them that—after all, Gallo was making an abundant Chablis Blanc and Hearty Burgundy many years ago—go into the Carlo Rossi bottles. I found the Chablis to be carefully made, tarter than C. K. Mondavi, and pleasanty sweet. Yosemite Road is Franzia's spin-off. Not nearly as well distributed as Carlo Rossi, it is, in fact, quite a discovery. At an even lower price, the Sauterne and some white varietals are flavorful even though a little thinner than the benchmark. But at these levels the benchmark is a little hard to remember! The third in this triumvirate is the product of the Bronco Winery, a consortium of "brothers and cousins" of the Franzia and Gallo families (bro 'n co). The "JFJ" stands for initials of those in the winery who decided to bottle the fermentations of other producers in the region. Here, two dollars and some change go a long way—all the way to three liters. The JFJ Chablis most recently on the market is dry enough, not nearly as fruity as the benchmark, but quite an accomplishment from this locale and at this price. These three "wineries" are within thirty miles of each other in that verdant triangle north of Modesto that claims a climate closer to parts of the North Coast than the interior valley. The results speak for themselves.

Everyday Wines: Rhine Type

Let us have wine and women, mirth and laughter
Sermons and soda water the day after.
—Lord Byron, Don Juan

The subject of Rhine wines brings to the fore the question of women's preferences. Through recorded history we have ample references to men and their flasks; could it be true that women were denied the full pleasures of the grape as it appears it was true of almost everything else? Women are certainly great appreciators of wines in our own day, but we don't see them on tasting panels or writing columns on anything but the uses of wine in cooking.

Several of California's wineries, some of them not so small, are guided by women enologists. Yet it's my impression that the vast majority of women lean to simple wines, and sweet ones at that. The popularity of the Rhine type—at most a distant relation to German Rhines—seems to have sprung mainly from the entry of women into the drinking market. My impression is confirmed every time I attend a wine tasting of the casual type conducted for both men and women: it's the sweetness that draws the women to Rhines.

We haven't had a Gallup poll on the subject, but a little observation will probably confirm that women prefer styles of wine different from those men like. Wine writer Pete Cockburn-Thorpe claims that at his frequent lectures and tastings the difference is unmistakable. In general, women lean to the whites, and to the whites with less dryness and as-tringency. Predictably, he notes that women assert their preferences only when they aren't tasting in the company of men! Most women apparently presume that men know what they're talking about, or even if women don't believe that, many feel it's better to humor the menfolk into believing that women are convinced of male savvy. The question that remains is whether women's preferences are simply a reflection of the neophyte's predilection for sweetness—or whether there is a basic physiological difference in their tastes.

If Lord Byron will allow me a morning-after sermon, I would like to entertain the possibility that much in men's tastes is socially conditioned and sometimes downright sexist. Our literature is replete with references to women and wine—in conjunction—as if both were simple objects of consumption. Since the time of Homer's wine-dark sea, Horace's odes to his beloved Falernian, the clinking of gourds and cups and the smashing of glasses in the middle ages, drinking wine thick as blood has been consid-ered a manly art. I'm reminded here of nutritionist Jean Mayer's remark that the blood-red steak is the motorcycle of the middle-aged man. Women have traditionally led the way to lighter foods, to fish, to vege-tarianism. Men often feel the need to put on a Henry VIII act at the dinner table. My point is that the male preference for the "big reds" may have less to do with the wine and more to do with the male psyche.

The wine critic of *The Washington Post*, William Rice, who has always had a very sensible attitude toward everyday wines, writes that California whites are becoming drier with each passing year. This must say some-thing about consumer tastes. Certainly the Tokays and Muscatels have fallen out of favor just about everywhere but skid row. Yet, at the same time, the Rhine types continue to flourish. Perhaps the two trends aren't contradictory.

One possible clue to the continued growth of sweet Rhines against the general swing to drier wines may lie in the epitome of the Rhine type: the varietals Gewürztraminer and Chardonnay. The former grape results in an extremely rich, almost syrupy wine of great complexity. To see what I mean, when you feel flush try a bottle of Chateau St. Jean or Louis Martini Gewürztraminer. Once a rarity in this country, there are now dozens of Gewürz labels coming out of California, mainly from the smaller, "boutique" wineries. The Berkeley Veedercrest winery exports its Gewürz to Germany, the home of auslese and spaetlese ("selected" and "late-picked") grapes. The Gold Medal and Grand Prize at the mammoth Los Angeles County Fair wine exposition in 1978 went to Smothers Gewürztraminer—yes, Tommy Smothers' second occupation in Sonoma. That means that out of eighty-one wineries presenting some 900 wines this was considered not only the best but the best product of all types. Now, what's wrong with the tremendous sweetness in these wines? As in the case of the much drier Chardonnays, there is enough fruit and sometimes wood flavor to establish a balance on the palate—but even then not for quaffing. I say that if a man (or a woman!) can quaff the richer, sweeter Rhine types without becoming sated with the sweetness, then there's enough balance of other elements.

As we will see, however, not *all* the wines labelled "Rhine" are terribly sweet at all—usually because there are other, quite sweet whites from the same maker. The guidelines from the California Wine Institute are no help: a Rhine, they say, should be "pale to medium straw-yellow in color, medium-bodied, or medium acid to tart, fresh and fruity." About the only difference between this description and that for Chablis is that the latter may be lighter in body. The truth is, of course, that most jug Rhines are simply sweeter versions of the chablis from the same maker.

The benchmark: Almadén Mountain Rhine. I have seen this Rhine version at more afternoon parties, bridge sessions, potluck suppers, and picnics that any other wine of any type. Perhaps I travel in strange company: one wine newsletter called it recently "a sweetish disaster,

Mountain Rhine is soft, slightly sweet, yet fresh and appetizing. It has a typical Rhine wine bouquet and the special lightness that makes such wines so agreeable. Here is a wine sure to please every-

ALMADÉN MOUNTAIN RHINE

one who likes Liebfraumilch. Mountain Rhine should be served chilled. It will go well with nearly every dish, although perhaps at its best with chicken, veal, fish, or cold meals in warm weather.

tasting somewhat of coffee beans," but then this critic sighs audibly whenever he's constrained to give a report on jugs. I disagree with the same critic's estimate that the label is misleading in describing it as "resembling in character and flavor a German Liebfraumilch." "Liebfraumilch" is a name used in Germany the way we use "Rhine" here—generic and sloppy identifications both. But the Almadén version has changed little over the years and reminds me of a wide variety of German wines.

On an earlier label, the main grape varieties used in its production were mentioned. One of them was the Burger grape. This may have endeared me to the wine for the wrong reasons. Then I discovered what the Burger grape is like—it ferments to almost complete dryness and has little more flavor than Thompson Seedless. Bob Ivie, the president of Guild Wines, once gave me some cuttings of the grape from his vineyards, remarking that it would be appropriate for me to make wine from it so that I could label it "Burger Burger." The results were as predicted—so dry and puckery that my friends always declined a second glass. At long last, however, I've discovered a use for it: Charles Crawford of Gallo informed me that this very dryness makes it an excellent blender in extra-dry champagnes!

In any event, Almadén Mountain Rhine will work well as a benchmark because of its consistency and easily identified components. It *is* sweet— but also quite rich in flavors typical of grapes in the Monterey-Salinas area. Its golden color matches these flavors well—altogether a well-rounded product that meets most people's tastes.

There's not the great variation in price among Rhines that there is in Chablis. The expensive Rieslings and Pinot Chardonnays, which might be matched in taste against Rhines, are better considered as "Sunday kind of jugs." And there are only a few very reasonable Rhines above the "Jugs Ordinaire" category; where price is a factor, it will be mentioned. Other-wise, the prices range between three and four dollars per 1.5 liter.

EVERYDAY RHINES FROM CALIFORNIA

Taylor California Cellars Rhine comes close to Almadén's version in its sweet finish and fruity, aromatic body. If you prefer a slightly crisper, less cloying version than the big benchmark, but still with plenty of substance, Taylor is a good choice. In the 750 milliliter size it's slightly more expensive than Almadén.

PAUL MASSON.
CALIFORNIA
RHINE

This is a wine of grace and delicacy—light and delicious. Its soft pleasing taste and clear gentle fragrance has a mysterious trace of sweetness reminiscent of spring flowers. Rhine should be well chilled and is a perfect companion to meals from the sea or afternoon outings. Produced and Bottled by Paul Masson Vineyards, Saratoga, California · Alcohol 11.5% by Vol.

1.5 Liters (50.7 fluid ounces)

PAUL MASSON (1859-1940)

Born in the Burgundy region, where his family had made wine for many generations, Paul Masson came to California in the 19th Century. Constantly an innovator, he pioneered in transplanting the choice wine grape varieties from France to his vineyards and created one of the first California Champagnes. Today, the premium wines, champagnes and brandies made by Paul Masson Vineyards are reflections of quality and tradition he himself established in almost a half century devoted to making fine wine.

If you want to move further to the dry side. Paul Masson Rhine is an excellent start. I've mentioned the Masson Emerald Dry; this vintner also has a Rhine Castle at the same, rather high price that aims squarely at those who prefer a rich, fully sweet product "resembling in character and flavor a German Liebfraumilch," to quote the Alamdén label again. The Rhine Castle seems to have a muscat flavor behind its sweetness—this is the top of the line if your tastes run in that direction. The plain Rhine, however, is quite dry while still retaining excellent body and bouquet. It's not one of those "discoveries" that cause a frenzied search around town by people who could well afford to pay an extra dollar a bottle—just standard Paul Masson quality. It tied for first in the Robert Balzer taste-off against Taylor, Gallo, Colony, and Mondavi mentioned in the Chablis section above. But again I caution against one-two-three rankings: on a scale of twenty the top three were within one tenth of a point of each other, and Almadén and Inglenook Navalle failed to reach the prize list. Meanwhile, a newsletter dismisses Paul Masson's version as not being of much interest.

Italian Swiss Colony seems determined to grow out of the "little old wine maker" image it created for itself in television advertising some years back. Now using simply the Colony label, it *has* achieved critical recognition to add to its popular appeal. Its version of Rhine is a case in point. Tending also to dryness, but with fresh fruit flavors in abundance, it's a match in every way for the Masson version with which it shared first honors in the Balzer tasting. To keep matters in perspective, the same critic who damned Paul Masson with faint praise referred to this wine as abysmal. That verdict is rather harsh against a wine so generous as this one. But you be the judge, if your tastes run to the tart side. Colony has a

sweeter version for you in their Rhineskeller Moselle; against the Almadén benchmark this one is clearly paler, less fruity, though equally sweet—a remove from the heavier side that may be what you want. I've included for consideration here also their Chenin Blanc, even though I mentioned that varietal also in the Chablis section. This one is sugary enough to match the Moselle from the same maker, but again a step removed in intensity. Colony, by the way, usually nets more change back for you at the cash register.

GALLO

RHINE WINE
OF CALIFORNIA

Our Rhine is a delicate dry wine—with a whisper of sweetness. This makes it most enjoyable with food. Made and bottled by the® Gallo Vineyards of Modesto, Calif. Alc. 11.5% by vol.

Also quite reasonable in price are C. K. Mondavi and Gallo, the latter with several entries in this category. As ever, Gallo seems to have gauged the public's taste accurately by presenting a slightly sweeter style in its Rhine, but thinner than Almadén. In its varietals, Sauvignon Blanc and Riesling might be considered Rhine types, though I've included the former and Chenin Blanc under Chablis. What's the difference? (Perhaps some day there should be a wine tasting in which the judges were asked to tell if they were drinking Chablis or Rhine types.) Gallo, as we will see, has been an important factor in upgrading the quality of varietals (not all Chenin Blancs or Sauvignon Blancs produce the same fruit, not to mention the same wines). The evidence is here in Gallo's subtle and quite distinct varietal wines.

I think the Inglenook Navalle Rhine is at the disadvantage of not having the same access to fruitier grapes, if I may call them that, than either Taylor, Almadén, Colony, or Gallo. The way grapes, grape concentrate, and fermented grape juice are trucked around California; only your winepresser knows for sure! In any case, the Navalle version is quite a modest offering, in spite of its sweet tooth. Yet it is smooth, unexceptionable, and crisp compared to the fruitier versions above. Again, the style of the maker is what counts: is the style to your liking?

Indeed, it's difficult to imagine any mass-produced wine nowadays to have glaring defects. Enologists and wine buyers and experienced tasters have too much control over the final product for disasters to occur. As we move to some of the very inexpensive Rhines, we might expect shortcuts and skimping—but not clumsiness.

The Franzia Brothers sold their winery near Manteca, California some years ago to Coca Cola, without any drastic change in operations visible to the travelers on their way to Yosemite who passed their tasting room (thus their secondary label, Yosemite Road). Californians have been familiar with the Franzia name for years, also, from the fact that PSA—Pacific Southwest Airlines, an intrastate carrier—has always served Franzia champagne as a complimentary gesture on its flights, thus lending meaning to its onetime slogan, "The Only Way to Fly." Franzia continues to produce popular, low-priced everyday wine in the shadow of its big brother Gallo, but without Gallo's consistency. Their Rhine is quite heavy in sugar and grapiness, without the roundness of Almadén's version—but if you like adventure the price is attractive. Under the Yosemite Road label, if you can get it at any great distance from their headquarters in the valley, the French Colombard qualifies as a tart Rhine type—even more economical.

Guasti Rhine is a step up in price, but still quite affordable. At the

ESTATE BOTTLED
WEIBEL
PREMIUM CALIFORNIA WINE
GREEN HUNGARIAN

The original winery was founded in 1869 and for three generations our family has made this delicately semi-sweet varietal wine It has a unique charm and versatility you will find most enjoyable as an aperitif and with virtually all foods Fred Weibel
PRODUCED AND BOTTLED BY WEIBEL CHAMPAGNE VINEYARDS, MISSION SAN JOSE, CALIF.
DISTRIBUTED WORLD WIDE EXCLUSIVELY BY THE FLEISCHMANN CO.,
NEW HYDE PARK, N.Y. • ALCOHOL 11% BY VOLUME

1978 Los Angeles County Fair it received a Second Award—the range of honors being from gold, silver, and bronze medals to awards and honorable mentions. Several or no awards may be made in each category. Like the other wines from the lower central valley, from Fresno to Bakersfield, Guasti shows more tartness and an earthiness that are not at all objectionable—especially when sugar is present, as in their Rhine. Cribari relies on the same general grape sources and produces a similar Rhine, price and all. It's worth mentioning an unusual varietal from the same area, Green Hungarian, made by Giumarra in Bakersfield. The price is certainly right when you consider the other Green Hungarians available in the state; but in sweetness and fruitiness this one is quite similar to the Rhines produced at the other end of the valley by the Franzias and Gallos.

Now we come to one of those cases of word-of-mouth wine-upmanship, or what might be called the power of the grapevine. Every now and then a wine will come along with these three characteristics: (1) it's cheaper than the other jugs; (2) it's recommended by at least one expert as being the equal of premium wines; and (3) it's at least passably drinkable. I say "at least" because many of these "finds" have stood the test of time—the most notable being Gallo Hearty Burgundy. Some years ago this same bolt of lighting struck Growers Rhine, though not with the attendant national publicity. Bars began to order it as house wines, some not caring to remember it was the Rhine they were supposed to order and not the Chablis or Chablis Blanc. Those types turned out to be quite acceptable, too, and Growers is now one of the largest selling jugs in the country—even if you can't find it at your favorite liquor store. Actually, the winery behind this trade name, Setrakian, has long been making wines for other bottlers, as was the case with Guasti and Giumarra. (In the same general area, at Arvin, California, the DiGiorgio family and its spin-offs continue to make wine for jugs shipped around the country. The large New York City retailer, Astor, has most of their house jugs made here—in varying qualities and prices. Their Rhines, for example, under the names "Astor Home," "Cromwell Vineyards," and "Como," are about $2.50 for the 1.5 liter size. In the same store I checked, the Almadén Mountain Rhine was a dollar more. This is the economics of buying other people's wine and labeling it yourself.)

Growers Rhine has the thinness in color and body characteristic of valley whites of this kind, but, with a nice balance of sweetness and acidity, it pleased anyone who had laid out a little more than two dollars for a gallon of it. Then came the revisionists—as they do to all historical subjects. One reviewer termed it "eminently unpleasant." The bars I have checked that first caught it in its high-flying days are, in the main, still supporters, but the search is now on for the next "find." Yet if there was ever a winery in which the spirit of the owners shows through, it's Growers—and the Setrakians.

Bob Setrakian isn't the wizened patriarch one has in mind in thinking of founding vintners. But then neither are many of the others—the Wentes, the Concannons, the Mondavis, the Gallos. Still well in his prime, he handles things at the Yettem, Tulare County, winery while his son Scott holds down the headquarters in San Francisco. Both are given to flamboyance and never take themselves too seriously—after all, the Setrakian name is seen only rarely on wine labels, mainly brandy and champagne.

Setrakian and Growers are the same company, with the "parent" concentrating on varietals and the offshoot on jug generics.

When they introduced their finest port to date they named it "Ouvre La Port," and in spite of this self-denigrating pun it promptly won a Bronze Medal at the Los Angeles County Fair. In all, the Growers Winery took twenty-six prizes at the fair—more than any other winery—all eighty of them—in 1978. Many of the prizes were for sherries, ports, champagnes, and brandies, but also among them were a Silver Medal and a First Award for Burgundies, a Bronze Medal for a Vin Rosé, and a Third Award for a Zinfandel. This eye-opening accomplishment must have emboldened the elder Setrakian to take a typically self-assured step—for he soon challenged the board chairman of Coca Cola, owner of Taylor, to a winner-take-all blind tasting of Growers versus the Taylor wines that appeared in the controversial taste-test TV ads. The loser would donate $25,000 to a scholarship fund. After a long delay, the only answer was that the situation was being evaluated. It was, nevertheless, an unprecedented offer that demonstrated, once and for all, the absurdity of ironclad claims in such a subjective thing as the taste of wine. As a neighboring vintner put it—Jerry

Stanners, president of Perelli-Minetti—"The use of a single comparative wine tasting as the basis for a claim of superiority misleads the consumer into believing what no experienced person in the wine business believes: that a comparative tasting can ever provide an absolute measure of quality."

When the Setrakian name is better known and their medium-priced wines better distributed, wine lovers will have the chance to give them at least a *comparative* measure of quality. Meanwhile, father and son continue to promote the line with such off-the-wall give-aways as a package of grape seeds entitled, "Grow a Grape and Step on it." Under "Instructions" the potential vineyard owner is told, "Choose a place with plenty of sun, near the Rhine River if you're close by. . . . 500 grape vines to an acre is normal and in five years your crop could be ready for harvest. At this point, call Bob Setrakian at California Growers Winery. Do not Mail Him The Grapes!"

Everyday Wines: Burgundy Type

The wine they drink in Paradise
They make in Haute Lorraine.
—G. K. Chesterton, A Cider Song

And in Yettem, and Ceres, and Plymouth, and Acampo, and Delano, and Vineburg. The California Burgundies are produced the length and breadth of the state. The Italianates, as one critic calls them, abound. But Frenchmen, Armenians, Germans, Spaniards, and even the English are in there pitching, too. The range of what passes for Burgundy is so great that this is the area for real discoveries: the search goes on for that little Italian place hidden in the foothills where grapes are crushed by hand (or foot!) and the wine is drawn straight from the lees for bottling.

Fred Cherry tells the revealing story of a German wine maker who was asked if the expensive estate and *auslese* wines could possibly be worth the price. The jovial fellow spread his arms as wide as if he was describing the fish that got away. "Price!" he said. Then he cupped his hands close together as if in prayer. "Quality." For the 1979 holidays wine lovers were told they would have to pay $50 or $60 for a bottle of Dom Perignon Champagne. A wine merchant retorted, "No bottle of anything is worth that much." Yes, the price range is equally dramatic in the big reds that we have traditionally known as Burgundies. The question is: How great or how small is the range of quality?

From what I've seen, the range is wider here than in the other types of jug wines. It pays to look for something out of the ordinary. Equally intriguing for the wine buff is the feeling—shared by many—that in this category price is very often no guide at all.

As I mentioned in the first chapter, I believe a trend is developing that will eventually result in two distinct kinds of everyday red wines, just as there are two whites. In one Burgundy tasting after another, I've seen certain fine wines dismissed as being too thin or sharp for the basic Burgundy attributes of mellowness and fullness. No doubt some thought went into Gallo's choice of the word "hearty" to describe its front-running Burgundy. They tell me that the word most often mentioned after that by the average wine drinker, when asked to describe what he thinks a Burgundy should be, is *mellow*. Well—where does that leave the clarets—so-called because the English public referred to the wines of Bordeaux as "clear" in color, in contrast to the blood-red Burgundies? It's true that the great châteaux of Bordeaux have long produced rich, full wines, but the general impression still remains that there is a certain bite, a steminess, and a crispness in the clarets in contrast to the bigger body of the Burgundies.

Therefore, I have taken many wines out of the Burgundy category to create a claret group. Many of the varietals, such as cabernets and Zinfandels, rightfully belong in the claret category (and not for the simple reason that Cabernet and Merlot are the grapes of the Bordeaux region of France). Especially in jug wines, where aging in or out of wood is often not feasible, these premium grapes yield lighter wines. Petite Sirah, Carignane, and Alicante are the red grapes for Burgundies; the "true" Burgundy grape, Pinot noir, is unaccountably fickle on California soil. And many of the new hybrids created to grow in the interior valleys of the state can go either way.

Consider the popular Ruby Cabernet. This is a marrying of Cabernet—for character—and Carignane—for durability in hotter climes. The result is a bountiful vine, unlike the niggardly Cab, which yields a fruity grape in the Cabernet manner. This is the label that most often perplexes wine shoppers: Is the "Ruby" just a proprietary word like "Hearty"? No—it's the name of the vine and the grape. Is the wine behind the label a real Cabernet, just different in color? No—it's a distinct type, something like the clarets of old. Many other promising hybrids have done well after five or more years in the Sacramento-San Joaquin Valley; cousins of mine near Woodland have turned their former sugar beet lands over to wine grapes with excellent results. Quite significant for other parts of the country is the development of a vine that can grow vinifera grapes even in the warmer climes of the Southeast; it's a cross between the wild muscadine of that region and several California varietals.

The explosion of all sorts of varietals in jugs, caused primarily by a glut of red (or black, as they call them in the trade) grapes, has in fact left many fine wines out in the cold in wine tastings. If you're going to judge Burgundies, you buy wines that say "Burgundy" on the label, right? Not so simple. The wine shopper faced by scores of red wines on the liquor store shelves isn't interested in the description on the label: taste and price are his main considerations. And the word "glut" is none too strong for the situation. In recent years wine masters have been able to set their price per ton and tell growers to take it or leave it—Cabernet, Zinfandel, or Carignane. More and more varietals are going to be bottled in jugs, and they're going to give the generics a run for their money. At the same time, the generics will contain higher percentages of the finer grape varieties. Distinctions in taste will be harder to make.

How, otherwise, could a winery put out a Burgundy and a Zinfandel at the same price? Unthinkable only a few years ago, this is now a commonplace. And, as I've already mentioned in connection with Chablis and Chenin Blanc, there's no reason why the varietal should automatically be better than the generic.

Here, then, is a first attempt at separating the huge array of red table wines into two camps, Burgundy and claret.

The Benchmark: Inglenook Navalle Burgundy. This wine surprised me and most of the tasters, amateur and professional alike, who sampled wines around the country in preparation for this book. It's definitely middle of the road, making it a good standard to measure such a huge field. But not middle of the road in quality. Of the entire Navalle line, this is the best evidence of continuing improvement in standards at this respected California institution. In a sense, it offers the characteristics that the beginning wine appreciator looks for: softness, a fairly light body with a touch of sweetness, finishing quite smoothly. There are no big surprises here; even the color and aroma are just what one would expect of a well-produced wine. It's not the type of wine that wins awards, though it does rate high in most published tastings.

As in the case of the Chablis, it helps to divide the field into three general price categories—which can overlap depending on the store, the time of year, the sense of urgency at the winery, and other imponderables!

HIGHER-PRICED BURGUNDIES

Navalle's big brother, the Inglenook North Counties line, offers a Vintage Burgundy that seems to have been built on the Navalle superstructure. Just breaking through the four dollar barrier for 1.5 liters, this bountiful wine represents quite an improvement for a few pennies a glass.

I have tried to avoid judgmental terms in comparing wines to the benchmark, but it's hard to resist here and in the following selections. Oak aging is evident in contrast to the Navalle, and the richness lingers in the mouth long after the wine has disappeared.

A newcomer to the Napa Valley scene, Franciscan worked hard at its fifths before introducing an everyday wine and reaped the reward: a Burgundy that has won so many awards it's hard to find it in the stores. To my taste it's closer the the Navalle in aroma and body, not quite as rich as the Inglenook above, but equally long lasting. Expect to pay a little more, too, if you can find it. This wine comes closest to my opinion—and memory—of a good French Burgundy, at least in style if not aging and complexity.

As in the Chablis category, Fetzer has produced a Burgundy type named simply for its color: Premium Red. If you've ever tried the Fetzer Carignane—the first time, to my knowledge, that a major vintner acknowledged this workhorse grape with its name on the label—you'll recognize an attempt here at quite a different wine. I understand the Premium Red is made completely from Carignane; but in this case it apparently has been refined enough to minimize some of the distinctive Carignane greenness. It's difficult to compare it to the Navalle except in richness: there is no sweetness in the Fetzer but about the same body. Not tasting them one after the other, it might be difficult to make any comparisons at all. In the end, the lower residual sugar of the Fetzer would seem to make it more drinkable away from the dinner table.

The wine that resembled Fetzer so much in style and even appearance in the Chablis is absent from this list. I've put Robert Mondavi's Red Table

California

RED TABLE WINE

ALCOHOL 12% BY VOLUME
PREPARED AND BOTTLED BY
ROBERT MONDAVI WINERY
OAKVILLE, NAPA VALLEY, CALIFORNIA
B. W. ⸱ CA. ⸱ 4802

A wine for everyday use made entirely of varietal wine grapes. Flavorful and complex in character.

Wine in the claret category. Until I did this I could never understand why these two fine products finished so far apart in blind tastings. Because they are different in style, the tendency is to try to see which one is "better." I think I've avoided that dilemma, and I hope my sense of taste is confirmed by the growing popularity of both labels.

There are at least two ways to treat a Zinfandel, that enigmatic grape whose ancestry is clouded in the haze of early California history. It does indeed have a "berry" nose, or simply *smell*, if you prefer. But usually this is lost in the oak aging and blending with other varietals. A young, 100 percent Zin can smell as if a raspberry patch were nearby, and it can be quite thin in body at the same time. In this case it ranks as a claret. Those Zinfandels that are treated in fermentation and aging as if they should be full and mellow I'll mention under the Burgundy heading, below.

MEDIUM-PRICED BURGUNDIES

All the major wineries produce one and sometimes as many as four wines that could be considered Burgundies, all in the everyday category and all similarly priced. Sebastiani's is similar to, but slightly "hotter" in body than the Navalle; its finish is accordingly sharper, and I would guess it has less residual sugar. The same winery's Zinfandel at a few pennies more per glass may be a purer breed, but without the zest. Colony Burgundy is another standby, fulfilling the promise of heartiness at an even lower price. The Chianti designation would seem to be more appropriate for an Italian wine maker, but in the case of Colony's version and most others this name is used for a thinner, younger, and much cheaper red. It may call up visions of grass-covered bottles and red and white checkerboard tablecloths, but I don't find any romance in the actual liquid. Neither of these Colony wines finish with the roundness of the Navalle. About C. K. Mondavi's entry there seems to be quite a division of opinion: wine critic Frank J. Prial calls it "one of the last of the old-style, full-bodied jug wines still widely available at a reasonable price," while Robert Finigan, in his meticulously thorough *Private Guide to Wines* newsletter, passes it by without comment. Differences of opinion in this field aren't unusual, but I think this one illustrates once again the difficulties of varying styles. The C. K. brand is a florid, let-it-all-hang-out act of wine making, quite welcome, in my opinion, from a major maker. Paul Masson's version of Burgundy is more sedate, lighter than the Navalle, too. Los Hermanos, the Beringer second line, also has an inoffensive thinness, with a characteristic touch of sweetness. I happen to be of the school that considers sugar to be the enemy of bold red wines, preferring them a little warmer than most that come from a cool closet or cellar; and I don't think this is an affectation when applied to everyday wines, either. But sweetness does help ":color" a lighter red, and there's no reason why such versions can't be downed with—forgive me, H. Warner Allen—ice cubes. Add to this Almadén's very similar product (even its Ruby Cabernet at a higher price is neither mouth-filling nor tart on the tongue), and you get a picture of a rather conservative, careful, if not to say bland offering of, supposedly, California's most basic wine. The public taste is not offended at all, but I think these are the wines that put off so many European critics—expecting, as they do, something more positive from a product carrying the noble Burgundy name.

Among the somewhat smaller wineries, like Pedroncelli, the Burgundies surpass the Navalle in body at the risk of roughness. Louis Martini announces its entry into this field with blood-red lettering of the name on its traditional label. It doesn't matter to me that the label doesn't say "produced" and hence indicates another winery's fermentation; the fact is the Martinis live up to their reputation here again for individuality. Their Mountain Red Wine is quite tart, perhaps not as sippable as the Navalle but quite authoritative on the dinner table. The same can be said for Foppiano's Burgundy and Zinfandel, priced the same and as full-bodied. Parducci's Burgundy is one of those rare cases in jug wines of a vintage-dated label. The 1974 there was made from grapes 95 percent of which were harvested in that year—that's all it means. Since 1974 was a good year in California (no late frosts, no thunderstorms after the fruit appeared on the vines, early sun and a consistent summer leading to a grape sugar of 25 Brix and an acid above .8), the '74 vintages can be expected to be big and flavorful, all other things being equal. This Parducci jug, compared with the Navalle, is indeed long on fruit and somewhat tart. The Geyser Peak Winery in Healdsburg shares the same general countryside with Ukiah's Parducci, so one might have expected their Summit Burgundy to be similarly full-bodied. It is, with a touch of sweetness close to the Navalle.

When we go to even smaller wineries, there seems to be an inverse proportion to the size of the wine. Three similar-sounding names of three widely dispersed wineries are often confused, because all three can be counted on in any year to come up with surprising reds: Barengo, Bertero, and Bargetto. The first actually prices its Zinfandel below its Burgundy—just in the order of body. I find the Burgundy especially to be in the authentic, old Italian manner, like the C. K. Mondavi only more so. Bertero's Zinfandel, on the other hand, happens to be more astringent than it Burgundy; an excellent wine for the money. And even less expensive is Bargetto's Ruby Cabernet, which outshines the Burgundy and Zinfandel from the same maker in richness and individuality. Minor "discoveries" all.

Some years ago a similar "discovery" appeared in San Francisco under the names Rege and Alfonso Rege "Private Reserve." (It should be noted that this last appellation, which has some meaning when applied to the products of the finer wineries, such as Beaulieu, is often used indiscriminately for the entire line of a jug maker. Valley of the Moon, mainly a local house wine, has a well-bodied "Private Reserve" Burgundy—their whole production!) Rege was sold mainly in gallon jugs, but when rumors started flying about this robust product it began to disappear into the

mansions of San Francisco's Pacific Heights. The blush is now off the rosé—and the Burgundy and Chablis, too—but it still has a loyal following and remains a good value. The late writer William Bronson, Denver Sutton, and I used to have periodic taste-offs of our current discoveries, agreeing that Rege would be our "control."

There is no reason why a larger winery than these cannot become a discovery, too. The classic example, which I'll come to shortly, is Gallo Hearty Burgundy. Another has recently hove into view, at least in the opinion of writers like Robert Balzer: Famiglia Cribari Mendocino Burgundy, priced dead-even with its more illustrious competitor. Like Gallo, Cribari offers the same everyday wine in fifths as well as 1.5 and 3 liters, so it's easy to sample. Sample it Balzer did; his reaction is an eloquent description of the fragile nature of aroma in a wine. Recalling that vines near paved roadways in France have been known to produce grapes with petroleum smells, he waxes poetic about the forest incense he perceives in the Cribari:

For years, we've nourished the belief that the forests surrounding the vineyards in Mendocino County lend an additional intrigue to the bouquet, drawn from the carpets of pine needles and cedar bark. . . . Among the functions of the leaves of the vines, those triple-pointed, deeply serrated shields that protect the berries from excessive sunlight, is more than mere photosynthesis and the development of natural grape sugars. . . . If the alien smell of tar can be transmitted into the grapes and then into the wine, is it not logical that the more pleasant incense of pine needles, haunting echoes from cedar or fir forests surrounding a vineyard, might also be drawn into the network of veins in the glabrous surface of the · leaves?

Albert Cribari, present wine master of the firm and grandson of the man whose face appears on every label, Beniamino Cribari, relates that his father would advise him on walks through the vineyards to be careful about planting other bushes and certain vegetables near the vines because of the effect they would have on the flavor of the grapes. It's no surprise, therefore, that the vineyards in the Monterey-Salinas area have a reputation for "vegetal" character: this is the largest artichoke and lettuce growing region in the country. Yet we mustn't look for alfala, or ghostlier, aromas in wines made near Ceres: Fred Cherry tells of a wine aficionado who talks about the color of the shirt of the picker. Let's not start hearing the echoes of his grunts as he moves among the lower vines. What about the taste of the wine? A blend of Carignane, Charbono, Alicante, and Grenache, it is indeed a rich offering—younger and sharper than our benchmark, but all this and pine needles for well under two dollars a fifth.

Going even further down the price ladder, if that seems possible, we encounter quite a bit of irregularity, but still enough character to keep them above "Jugs Ordinaire." I have mentioned Yosemite Road favorably among the whites; here it is even more of a pleasant surprise—with the Cabernet, if you can ever find it, priced right along with the Burgundy. I first encountered the Cab at a potluck supper and couldn't believe my eyes when I saw $1.99 marked clearly on the bottle—a gallon! The whole Yosemite Road line has since disappeared from the outlets I frequent, no doubt because various newsletters also picked up on this Act of God. The mistakes occur when an otherwise good winery attempts to cater to what it perceives as an ethnic or special market of some kind, instead of sticking to sound wine making. Villa Armando has an unusual jug, which I have seen in various parts of the country, called Rustico. The label advises that the natural alcohol of the wine has been boosted up to 16 percent by the use of brandy, and the sugar of the grapes to begin with was quite high in the warm Livermore Valley where the winery is located. This is one way to make a "big" wine! I would rather call it a beverage—not at all unpleasant from time to time, and certainly popular among hearty drinkers. Plenty of bang for the buck is also promised by an Eleven Cellars jug fetchingly named Farm Workers Pure Country Burgundy. I haven't been able to locate a bottle, but Robert Finigan wonders whether the wine is "a greater disservice to the labor movement or to the natural food craze." Knowing the other California Wine Association offerings fairly well, I would trust the FWPCB to be characteristic of interior valley reds and the victim of a swinging door with that moniker. Bertero has, I think, done something of the same thing in its Vino Mio, a cheap but oh so sweet thrill. Even here, however, I use the word "cheap" in no derogatory sense. The winery knows something about its market, and it has proved it can make wine to *my* tastes. The mistake, as I see it, is in not concentrating on the wines that are best suited to the average table; there is, after all, a shortage of raisins.

GALLO

HEARTY BURGUNDY

OF CALIFORNIA

We are often told by knowledgeable people that they are delighted in having discovered a great wine in Hearty Burgundy. Its rich, full-bodied flavor—from extremely fine varietal grapes—will surprise you. Alc. 12.5% by vol. Made and bottled by the ®Gallo Vineyards of Modesto, Ca.

I have saved three well-known favorites for last, because they are, in a sense, a transition to the next section. Gallo Hearty Burgundy has been the victim of Wine Critics' Revisionism in recent years: they say it seems to have lost some of its heartiness or is just plain boring. This was a common complaint quite soon after it attained national acclaim as the "best buy" in a *Consumer Reports* taste test. The demand was so great, everyone said, that Gallo couldn't maintain the quality. (That taste test, incidentally, included a Château Lafite-Rothschild! Comparing American with French wines is inviting but pointless—unless, as is the case with Robert Mondavi's

1974 Cabernet, the American wines are styled with that in mind.) The truth of the matter is, I suspect, that Gallo Hearty Burgundy is pretty close to what it always has been; the competitors have simply come aboard with their own fuller versions. The Model A of American red table wines, as Frank J. Prial dubs it, Hearty Burgundy shouldn't be expected to overwhelm you. It's bigger than the Navalle we're using as the benchmark, has a deeper hue, a little more aroma, and a little sharper finish. And it's still winning honors against everyday wines costing a third more. This brings us to the more expensive Taylor and Christian Brothers, with which Gallo Hearty Burgundy is often compared these days.

Alone among the premium California wineries, the Christian Brothers never issue a vintage-dated wine—meaning merely that they prefer to blend from year to year. Uniformity is therefore one of their hallmarks, no matter what the weather or the frost. These qualities would seem to give them an edge in entering the jug wine market. I find this to be the case, especially in color and finish, which must result from superior aging. You will have to pay more than you might expect for a jug to get these subtleties—so it all comes down to how *you're* using the wine: for company, for casual drinking, for quaffing. Compared to the Navalle, I see a general drift to lightness, which is also evident in the Burgundy from Taylor. There is no sharp dividing line between a California Burgundy and what I call a claret, but I think these last two are crossing no man's land. More cabernet, or at least ruby cabernet, is evident in both. When two excellent wines such as these fall out of favor in wine tastings, as they sometimes do, one has to wonder what the standards of the tasters are. My selection of wines for the claret category will make this point more directly.

Everyday Wines: Claret Type

*In the souls of the people the grapes of wrath are
filling and growing heavy for the vintage.*
—John Steinbeck, *The Grapes of Wrath*

A hypothetical Wrath Vineyards with a lot of red grapes on its hands has a problem most consumers never think about: what to name the wine. The different varietals are fermented separately, of course, in the huge redwood (in California) or stainless steel tanks one always sees in wine tours. The wine master has innumerable options after that: to let certain ones age further, to prepare others for bottling as varietals, to blend others with previous vintages, or to attempt any number of blends with the current vintages. If Wrath Vineyards has the normal laboratory, the residual sugar and acid content after fermentation is complete will be systematically recorded and tested as the lees settle. Then, how much refining to remove particulate matter? How much oak aging? Even if a wine-in-the-making is predominantly of a single grape variety, Wrath Vineyards may decide, on marketing principles, to call it a Burgundy or a claret so as not to upset their wholesalers and ultimately their customers. (A restaurateur I know samples every case of his house wine in the certain knowledge that his supplier eventually will have added a "gift" to his usual generic concoction. One winery I am familiar with was able to substitute Cabernet for the Ruby Cabernet in its Burgundy one year simply because of the surfeit of red grapes.)

Many of the words Wrath Wineyards has at its disposal to put on its labels are purely arbitrary—especially if it has played fast and loose with nomenclature in the past. Claret is such a name. But as it becomes more common, consumers are beginning to associate qualities with it, as they now associate "hearty" and "mellow" with Burgundy. In the meantime, I feel there's no reason to continue to lump all the reds under Burgundy or simply Red Table Wine.

Having given some of the lighter, more acidic, drier red wines a new category, perhaps we won't feel inclined to criticize them as having lost body, or having become sharp, or having become puckery. Maybe the reason why "the strawberries will never taste so good again" is that other things now taste different, that other things now occupy our palate. Here, at any rate, are my nominations for reds that don't have to compete against Burgundies, but can be just the wines they are.

The Benchmark: Italian Swiss Colony Cabernet Sauvignon. Balance is the key word here. Don't expect the oak you get from a Robert Mondavi or any of the smaller, newer cabernet makers. There are few rough edges, but there is also an underlying acidity that would be out of place in a Burgundy the way we view it. Strangely, the Pinot Noir—the grape of the Burgundy region—from Colony is even more like a French claret: thinner, with more bite and expressiveness in its flavor. But both are worth a try if the claret style is to your taste.

EVERYDAY CLARETS FROM CALIFORNIA

We might as well start with those wineries who have taken the trouble to label their clarets as such. Unfortunately, there are few guidelines and little consistency under this label designation. The small Plymouth winery of d'Agostini has a Claret with excellent balance of acids with low sugar. One would hardly expect a winery in the Gold Country to produce something to match a cabernet in the North Coastal region, but there it is. And it's also quite a bargain—well under three dollars for 1.5 liters, perhaps less in the store distribution area near the winery. But you have to keep a sharp eye out for it. As we will see in chapter 6, the d'Agostini wines are handled according to that H. Warner Allen maxim, "Those wines are best which owe least to human intervention."

The C. K. Mondavi Claret I found smoother but less complex than the benchmark wine, and not quite the bargain as above. I see this one as sort of a way station between a rosé and a Burgundy, if you're proceeding in the usual experimental fashion from lighter wines to richer ones.

Paul Masson's Rubion Claret, at about the above price level, is typically well finished and dry; I would even put Masson's Baroque Burgundy here, so lacking is it in those heavier characteristics of the well-known Burgundy jugs. The slight astringency in both make them easy to take over a long afternoon or evening.

The Christian Brothers Claret is firmly in the astringent camp of reds, lighter than the benchmark wine, but the highest-priced so far.

Giumarra's Breckenridge Cellars is the only winery to my knowledge to have won an award—in this case a Gold Medal at the 1978 Los Angeles County Fair—for a claret at an everyday price. By secondhand reports I understand that this fine wine is smoother and lower in acidity than the above, and of course it's an excellent value.

The claret offered by Growers is thinnest of all, without the varietal character apparent in many of the foregoing, with a touch of sweetness that seems out of place. It's something like the "little wines" or "new wines" meant to be drunk quite young—the weakest in the Growers' line, in my opinion—yet a lucky buy for you if it's to your taste.

In a recent tasting of fifteen California "Jug Reds," I noticed that all but two of the top nine were of the claret character, though under other names, and all but one of the bottom six were labeled Burgundy. Surely the weight of opinion among those tasters that day ran to a thinner type of red. At the top was Robert Mondavi's Red Table Wine, at the fanciest price and the subject of much disagreement among critics. Among the tastings I conducted, the words that best summed up this carefully made product were, "Stability, character, easy to stay with." There's clearly a cabernet feeling here, quite similar to the benchmark wine.

The Zinfandels in jugs also fit easily into the claret category: Foppiano (one of the lowest-priced), C. K. Mondavi, Los Hermanos, Inglenook Navalle, and Barengo. It's no accident that these clean wines finished in the top seven in the above-mentioned tasting. There are slight differences between them as varietals, especially Barengo with its greater acidity, but I think they should be viewed simply as lighter reds, drier than Burgundies. It would be pointless to catalog the dozens of other Zins, Ruby Cabernets, and even Cabernets now coming on the market in jug sizes that aim at this style of red. If you are lucky to find one with oak aging, or a dryness and astringency to your taste, make a note of it. It's a fast-changing field.

Everyday Wines: Rosé Type

It is WRONG to do what everyone else does—namely, to hold the wine list just out of sight, look for the second cheapest claret on the list, and say, "Number 22, please."
—Stephen Potter, *One-Upmanship*

Rosés were once thought of as the compromise wines. I introduced my wife to California wines on our honeymoon with a bottle of Paul Masson's Vin Sec Rosé, with excellent results. Hostesses often opt for rosé in fear of some gauche choice that would offend their more knowledgeable guests.

Fence sitters start with a good rosé and see no reason to move left or right. It was also once thought to be a deft example of one-upmanship to decline rosé whenever proffered and, like Stephen Potter's model, to order more exotic-sounding concoctions whenever faced with a wine list.

Upon examination one must conclude that rosés *are* safe choices; both whites and reds offer far more opportunities to make costly mistakes. Yet rosés, or pinks, to be consistent, are not merely halfway houses, neither fish nor foul, as some critics are always lamenting. They do have varietal characteristics, objective standards, and propensities for specific menus. Toulouse-Lautrec, who considered eating and drinking to be intimately associated with painting, was particularly fond of the pink Tavels and d'Anjous of his countryside while he was engaged in sketching nudes.

The Grenache grape was once the only one used in making a true rosé—that is, one with varietal characteristics. As I have mentioned in chapter 1, the abundance of premium red grapes in recent years in California has brought this innocent era to a close. We now have rosés of Cabernet and Zinfandel and all sorts of Cab and Zin Blancs that don't quite make it to the white stage and must be considered pinks. Unfortunately, few of these will ever become everyday wines at the prices we are considering here. The vinification needed to arrest the full red development of a Cabernet and refine it to a near-white wine make these fairly costly affairs. Recently a friend of mine ran out of his jug whites at a party he was hosting and felt required to turn loose on his guests a case of Sterling Cabernet Sauvignon Blanc worth about fifty dollars a case.

The University of California at Davis has devised a method of wine tasting that could be a boon to rosés in open competition with whites: completely black wine glasses. With these otherwise standard glasses, tasters cannot tell if the wine is the color of bourbon. Once the prejudice against color (here as in everything) is removed, the subjects can be evaluated simply on their merits. Unfortunately, too many vintners seem to go out of their way to sweeten their rosés to excess, as if to say "the color is already off, why not the flavor?" Many vintners also make their rosés the way some airline stewardesses do—by mixing whites and reds. Yet there remain enough good choices to make it worth your while selecting a rosé carefully.

A word of advice to the "fence-sitter" type of rosé drinker: You may be avoiding an ocean of beautiful wines just because you got knocked down once by the surf. I've known many wine buffs who went for years without ever trying a good red wine because the first few they attempted were sweet, temple-pounding horrors.

The Benchmark: Gallo Mountain Vin Rosé. Gallo has always taken its rosés quite seriously. I'm not sure what the Grenache content is nowadays, but the color indicates a cleanness in the varietals employed: the blush on a cheek rather than the pink of a faded stop sign. Sweetness is under control in the pleasant blend of fruity aromas and substantial body for a light-colored wine. This surely must be one of Gallo's most broadly appealing wines.

EVERYDAY ROSE WINES

My sentimental favorite, Paul Masson Rosé, as it is now more simply named, isn't the cheapest of the lot but has much to recommend it. To my taste the level of dryness is critical. Without Gallo's color, this wine does a lot with careful balance of lighter elements. I see no real difference between this and a good, dry Rhine—with eyes closed.

Also on the lighter side are Inglenook's Navalle and C. K. Mondavi's. Richness of color returns as we go further south in the northern wine-growing regions: notably Taylor California Cellars Rosé and Almadén Mountain Nectar Vin Rosé. The latter is characteristically on the sweet side for this vintner; the former stresses a bigger grape flavor with some tartness. The Taylor version is a rosé any red-wine drinker can appreciate.

Price is a factor to be considered with the inexpensive Los Hermanos product. I find it an equal match for fruit and astringency with Taylor, though the richness of color is somewhat lacking. Against Gallo I would say this is another case of a little more daring on the part of this St. Helena winery, "son of" Beringer.

The rosés of the large wineries in the interior valley to the southern part of the state seem to produce uniformly sweet aftertastes. The Franzia and JFJ Wineries also lean in this direction. Nor do I think they come near the attractive hues of the Gallo benchmark.

A pleasant surprise is always the rare discovery of a small winery offering more than a pink in its rosé. Such is the case at Rapazzini, so close by San Martín near Gilroy, California that visitors to the latter's tasting rooms often find themselves by mistake in the much smaller quarters of this family-owned and operated establishment. Rapazzini's Grenache Rosé is everything that the varietal name announces: fruitiness with a tart overtone and brilliant color. Good as it is, the benchmark version may seem pale if compared to this one in the same tasting. In reality, of course, it's the grape that makes the difference. The Los Angeles Country Fair awarded Rapazzini a Bronze Medal for this effort in 1978.

Parducci's Mendocino County Vintage Vin Rosé captured a First Award at the same event. Once again, note the unusual combination of a vintage year with a generic wine—and on a lighter wine, to boot. Since aging is usually a factor only with red wines and the big whites, such as

Pinot Chardonnay, it seems odd to "date" a rosé. The general opinion is that freshness is the key to most of California's nonred wines. In this case, the fullness and extraordinary color of the rosé apparently called for some bottle aging.

The Sebastiani Mountain Vin Rosé and Mountain Grenache Rosé are both offered at the same reasonable price, yet there is a noticeable difference in style between the generic and the varietal. I find the generic bolder and brighter than the Grenache, and a good contrast with the Gallo benchmark. There's no hint of purple in the Sebastiani hues; the fruit is clear in the aroma and on the palate; sugar is pleasantly absent. The Sebastiani Grenache seems to come closer, if anything, to Gallo, but there is still quite a bit more tartness in the former. Interestingly enough, a Sweet Rosé—a very honest name—was entered by Sebastiani and took a Gold Medal at the Los Angeles County Fair mentioned above. It's not generally available as an everyday wine.

The Sebastiani flair for robust generics and multitudinous varietals in jug wines is all the more surprising when one remembers that Sam J. (the grandson of the founder Samuele) and his father August were producing wines mainly for other bottlers in the East not too long ago. Sam takes pride in personally writing his firm's engaging monthly newsletter, as well as putting the Sebastiani touch on the production. Frank J. Prial paints a homey picture of the Sebastiani operation that sums up the success story of this and many other family wineries in California: as August watches his bottling lines "clank on through the night, he shakes his head in disbelief and says: 'I don't know what we're doing, but we're obviously doing something right.' "

3

Jugs Ordinaire

Forsake not an old friend, for the new is not comparable to him. A new friend is like new wine; when it is old you will drink it with pleasure.

—Ecclesiastes

The rule for the lower limit of price in a wine should be this: Unless it's good, you won't drink it daily. If you don't drink wine more than once or twice a month, forget the rule. Take somebody else's opinion and spend more to be sure of what you're getting. But if you are an adventurer and like to discover goodies for yourself—perhaps I should say if you are a *gambler*—now listen.

Twenty-five years ago I used to play a game called "Mountain Castle Roulette." Because wine isn't sold in grocery stores in many eastern states—for reasons unclear—you may not have heard of Mountain Castle wines. They're the house wines of Safeway Stores. It doesn't say "Scotch Treat" or "Townhouse" or "Busy Baker" on the label, but you know instinctively as soon as you see the label that it's a captive brand.

The game consisted of selecting a gallon jug at random from the many lining the lower shelves and risking something like $1.69 to see if it was (a) unbearable, (b) passable, or (c) drinkable with heavy food. Every now and then along would come a mistake: a white would be dry and acidic, a red would be dry and full-bodied. Then you would invite a friend over for a taste of your discovery and show the price on the label. As I recall, the whites were a better gamble, for the reds always seemed to have that characteristic valley sweetness that to me is cloying.

Nowadays the gamble is not a bad one at all, for two reasons: the "secondary" wines that go into these jugs are better than ever because of great strides in quality control, and the price has gone up only another dollar a gallon! I find an interesting contrast between western and eastern (United States) morality in the fact that you can use credit cards to buy food, but not wine, in many eastern states, but to buy wine, and not food, in western states. At any rate, this chapter is for you if you have the opportunity to purchase wine in your corner grocery: the low store-wine price induces a form of competition that brings other jugs into liquor stores at comparable bargains.

Other supermarket house wines I'm aware of are La Mesa (Safeway) and Harvest (Lucky Stores). Red Mountain, made by Gallo, is widely available in supermarkets. Liquor stores and even department stores in some part of the country, such as Macy's, have their own brands too—but these are generally equivalent to the lower levels of wine in the previous chapter. Continue to remind yourself that price is no certain measure of quality but also remember that a bargain doesn't gather dust on the shelves. Is there any way to make sense out of the bargain-basement wines? Or do you just have to gamble?

You can do some calculated guessing by reading the label a little more closely. By law, the location of the bottler—not necessarily the producer—must be shown. There are no wineries in San Francisco these days, yet many jug wines show a San Francisco address. And most of these "bottlers" aren't even listed in the telephone book. They are simply brokers doing business under names that sound like wineries, buying fermented wine from a winery, perhaps aging it somewhere else, and packaging it in a third place. The large producers of these anonymous wines, however, often choose to market their own products but under the label of a liquor store, grocery store, or dba. So the location of the winery appears on the label. And generally there is only one large winery in any of the small cities in the California central valley or north coastal region. Therefore, the label of a strange brand can be fairly reliably matched up with a winery as follows:

Modesto:	*Gallo*
Ripon:	*Franzia*
Ceres:	*Bronco*
Lodi, Fresno:	*Cribari (Guild)*
Manteca:	*Delicato*
Yettem:	*Growers (Setrakian)*
Arvin:	*DiGiorgio*
Bakersfield:	*Giumarra*
Los Angeles:	*San Antonio*
Delano:	*California Wine Association (Perelli-Minetti)*

Healdsburg:	*Geyser Peak*
	or Foppiano
Elk Grove:	*Gibson*
Hollister:	*San Benito*

When Hugh Johnson, the respected English wine authority, said that California jug wines are "vastly superior" to European *vin ordinaire,* I'm sure he wasn't referring to "jugs ordinaire." The anonymously produced wines from the above locations are generally products that don't stand up to the quality each of these wineries offers under its own name. Not that the wines are "off": vinegary or oxidized. They are simply made from grapes with insufficient acid, poor flavor concentration, or nontraditional wine tastes. One can make wine from any type of grape, but Concords make better grape jam or grape juice and Thompson Seedless makes better raisins or eating grapes. From another point of view, the "traditional" tastes expected in a wine (meaning the tastes associated with the *Vitis vinifera* grapes of Europe and chiefly of California in the United States) are also a factor of the art of the wine maker and aren't a sine qua non of wine enjoyment, anyway. From the way critics recoil in horror from the innocent Thompson Seedless one would think they were possessed like Coleridge's Ancient Mariner:

> Like one that on a lonesome road
> Doth walk in fear and dread.
> And having once turned round walks on,
> And turns no more his head;
> Because he knows a frightful fiend
> Doth close behind him tread.

Albert Cribari honestly describes his Extra Dry Chablis as a blend containing 75 percent Thompson Seedless. The grape matures early in the warm interior valleys—each vine heavy with fruit and each berry heavy with water. One need only sample a small, black cabernet berry in the vineyard and realize why the flavors of a Cabernet Sauvignon wine are generally so concentrated. Yet with patient vinification Cribari has achieved a relatively high acid level of .75 and a nice balance with the residual sugar of the typical valley grape.

Another much-maligned grape is the muscat. At one extreme in its history one could not enunciate the name without thinking of Muscatel and "winos." Then it was associated with pop wines like the "bird": "What's the word?" "Thunderbird!" "What's the price?" "Thirty twice!" But it has also given us such lovely things as Muscat Frontignan, Muscato Amabile, and the Christian Brothers Chateau LaSalle. D'Agostini has a very pleasant jug under a dry Muscat label. Like a Concord, however, the muscat seems to show its true colors in its natural sweet form, and given care it can be a delicious dessert *digestif*.

There are some low-priced jugs I have saved for comment here rather than in the previous chapter, not because they are as variable as some of the ones listed above, but because they are generally the cheapest large-volume jugs available in liquor stores around the country. C. C. Vineyards should be around two dollars for the new 3-liter size just about anywhere; the label tells you it's a Bronco wine (Ceres), and so a close cousin to the Franzias and Gallos. The whites I've tasted have been thin and somewhat biting, but not bad at all for extended drinking. A Vin Rosé that came out in 1978 perplexed a lot of people, including supposedly knowledgeable liquor store buyers. It was apparently made from black grapes taken off the skins early in the fermentation process, something like a rosé of Cabernet, but everybody expected one of those light, fairly sweetish wines we have come to expect from the valley. In most stores it was quickly marked down for rapid outward movement! The C. C. red is strangely thin, like a thrice-pressed country wine of France, but it is certainly drinkable and I have nothing against it as a cooler.

A friend of mine, Ray Thierry, used to make a "new wine" at his father's winery in Bordeaux by sugaring the last pressing of the must and adding water—the original wine cooler. Italy and California don't allow the addition of sugar, mainly because in their latitudes grape sugar is quite abundant. But many of the "jugs ordinaire" have that "new wine" taste.

One of the old standbys over the years in the low-priced category is Vino da Tavola, or simply Tavola. The distinctive checkerboard-tablecloth label accurately hinted that this was intended to be a full-bodied, old-style Italian picnic or luncheon wine. And it is—though it seems to me that so much has happened to the quality of other jug wines at a little extra cost that Tavola has now been relegated to the "ordinaire" category, by comparison. If you don't mind a sweetish aftertaste (it evaporates in the outdoors!), Tavola is certainly a consistent choice for you.

I have mentioned Vintner's Choice in the second chapter, but there is so much overlapping in prices from one store to another of the "everyday" wines with the "ordinaire" wines that I think it deserves mention here also. With Tavola and C. C., it's one of the few remaining jugs that attempt to compete at the general price level of the house brands. Often any of these will be touted by a "wineau" (Fred Cherry's term for a self-proclaimed wine authority, like myself) as having come from the same spigot as one of the higher-priced jugs from the same winery. My translation of this recommendation is that the wineau has lost some of his taste buds. Though the differences may seem small after a few sips, the large question is how well the cheaper version wears on one. Slight excesses in taste become magnified over a period of time; the flush of alcohol makes all wines brothers in the first few glasses. *At this level.*

Vintner's Choice Chablis may seem to be about the same as its big brother, Cribari's Vino Blanco, for a glass or two. Then the effects of sweetness begin to appear in the former. These two wines are offered off and on at that greatest bargain in the world for house wines, Tadich Grill in San Francisco. I don't know how long they can continue to pour a tumbler for 50 cents, but, while they do, it's more a public service than a business.

Perhaps the best commentary on whether any of these "ordinaires" will be sufficiently to your taste to drink on a daily basis is the state of wine appreciation at loftier levels. Among the more expensive wines is there any great unanimity of opinion? As it happens, there's something of a domino effect among wine critics. They watch the awards at county fairs and wine societies. They read each other's newsletters. Yet every now and then they review a wine simultaneously, with surprising results. Fred Cherry noted the following two opinions about the same wine, the same vintage, the same producer in two national magazines:

Expert No. 1: "... a stunner with its dark hue, blackberry jam bouquet, rich taste. ..."
Expert No. 2: "... unpleasant acetate overtones, little merit in the taste ... poor wine. ..."

My recommendation is to take the plunge at the lowest levels. If you blow a couple of bucks on something that leaves you gasping, console yourself with the thought that you can use it in cooking and marinating. (Caution: don't think you'll get good vinegar from a poor wine. Good vinegar, like good champagne, is based on the wine you begin with.) White wine is fine for marinating fish to make a ceviche or fish salad, as we will see in chapter 7. We usually think only of marinating pot roasts, but almost any meat, including chicken, improves by spending some time soaking up wine. A red wine that's too sweet for your taste should be excellent as a mulled wine. And you can also just throw it out, consoling yourself with the fact that it was cheaper than bottled water to begin with. Throwing things out, like sending a dish back to the kitchen, is a therapeutic ennoblement of the spirit that should not be denied to anyone who collects too many things and eats too much because of a niggardly childhood.

And then, it's always possible that you may make a lifelong friend. Twenty-five years later, I came back to Mountain Castle to discover that I could still drink it with pleasure, and that the mountains and valleys I had traversed in the meantime were neither all that low or high.

4

A Sunday Kind of Jug

Quinquireme of Nineveh from distant Ophir
Rowing home to haven in sunny Palestine,
With a cargo of ivory,
And apes and peacocks,
Sandalwood, cedarwood and sweet white wine.
—John Masefield, *Cargoes*

Monsiéur Lautrec, to whom we owe the phrase "a peacock's tail in the mouth" to describe a rich and fruity Burgundy, reserved the denunciation, for people whose taste he abhorred, "They are not worthy of ring doves with olives, they will never have any, and they will never know what it is."

To describe with feeling the experience of tasting a noble wine, we must work ourselves up to such heights of similitude, even if it be a jug. Not all the treasures are at the ends of tree-lined roads, and not all the wines of elegance are festooned with etchings of châteaux. Let our language echo the sentiment and pleasures of even a casual glass of good wine. Thus were born toasts.

Among the jugs the most surprising discovery of quality, I feel, is in the sweet dessert wines, golden and amber and burnished bronze. Not too many of the best are in jugs, per se; but they fulfill our definition of being drinkable everyday, or, should we say, every Sunday? Listen to some of the names: Angelica, Sherry de Oro, Cream Marsala, Ambermint, Muscadelle du Bordelais, Muscat Canelli, Triple Cream Sherry, Fin de Nuit, Tinta Madeira Port, Black Muscat, Almondoro, Malvasia Bianca. Then there are the fruit wines, either flavored with extract or fermented from fruit with the help of sugars from grapes: Strawberry, Apricot, Plum, Peach, Blackberry, and Old Fashion American Apple; Mint and Coffee; Chocolate; and the familiar Sangria. The experts raise their noses at these as aberrations to please the uneducated palate; yet the same principle is involved in the delicate German May wines, flavored with woodruff, and, more commonly, in vermouth. Those who would dismiss Gallo's very pleasant Spanñada merely because it is not *completely* a fermented wine have a quarrel with Martini and Rossi.

If I may stretch the definitions a bit, I would like to mention the dessert wines of Llords & Elwood. By no stretch of the imagination are these within jug wine prices, but the labels are within jug wine spirit! In several tastings I have seen, and private evaluations, Llords & Elwood Great Day D-r-ry Sherry has sacked Dry Sack hands down, and their The Judge's Secret Cream Sherry has overruled Harvey's Bristol Cream. The importance of these findings is not so much in the betterment of Llords & Elwood, but in the compliment by analogy it gives to the entire California dessert wine field. Llords & Elwood has no monopoly of traditional techniques, modern technology, or good grapes among California vintners.

Today, the excellent sherries and ports of Almadén, who pioneered the solera method in California among the popular makers, can be bought reasonably in jugs; meanwhile, their fifths (or 1.5 liters) are hardly out of line with everyday drinking standards. The same is true of Beringer, Cresta Blanca, Inglenook, and Christian Brothers. I'm not going to try to establish any benchmarks in this polymorphous field, except to point out a few brands that have stood the test of time and critical opinion.

Gallo Livingston Cream Sherry, named after the location of one of Gallo's three wineries, is one of the great bargains in dessert or any wines. Not quite as rich as Almadén's Solera Cream, it's under three dollars for 1.5 liters and will give any imported cream sherry a run for the money. Magnums of Cresta Blanca's Triple Cream Sherry are between six and seven dollars—well into the price level of a Sunday wine—but quite an experience for sherry lovers. I haven't mentioned the much cheaper brands, and there are quite a few, because I believe they are mainly useful for cooking and in certain mixed drinks where taste comparisons are academic. This is only my opinion; namely, that a wine meant for sipping is worth spending a little more on. So far, the only case I have found where price doesn't correlate directly with quality is the Gallo mentioned above. A good middle-of-the-line choice for all dessert wines that will never let you down is Paul Masson, at about four dollars per 1.5 liters.

I don't mean to imply that Sunday is sweet wine day; I am just thinking of that Italian tradition of bringing out the very special wine on great feast days, Easter, etc. Pietro Pinoni, whose book *How to Make Wine Like My Grandfather Did in Italy* is a charming, short introduction to the old school of wine appreciation, recalls that his grandfather always seemed to have a sweet white wine, such as Malvasia Bianca or Muscato, in reserve for St. Peter's Day. Perhaps champagne is the wine we consider reservable nowadays for special occasions. Here some of the eastern wineries, such as Taylor and Great Western, compete very favorably with Californians. The problem I see so often is that the poor consumer has few options in the choice of champagne, in spite of all the brands. The house champagnes of liquor stores and one or two major low-priced brands, such as Le Domaine, run under three dollars a fifth, especially if you can find them in magnums. Then all the rest are above four dollars, usually bunched around five dollars. The sleeper in the champagne field is Setrakian—if you can find it. It doesn't come in magnums, but it is priced right between these two extremes—at around three dollars or a little more. There are two surprises about Setrakian champagne: it comes in an elegant, French-type bottle with a thin neck and deep base, and it is a wonderfully dry champagne (Brut). You can have Cold Duck, Sparkling Burgundy, or Pink Champagne in the same bottle, but I find these pseudo-champagnes to be a poor compromise between pop wine and a truly Sunday kind of wine.

The still able wines—white, red, and rosé, unfortified wines—can put' on their Sunday best, too. I have already mentioned a few of these in chapter 2 at the upper end of the price range, notably Robert Mondavi Red Table Wine and Fetzer Premium Red. Whether those and a few others should be considered in that category or here is purely arbitrary as far as price is concerned. A few of them warrant mention as Sunday wines because they have characteristics that make them worth saving for a special occasion during the week—even though they may be priced at or slightly below the two reds mentioned above.

The Robert Mondavi Rosé Table Wine is a good example. It's the same price as the red and the white, but there are many other rosés at lower prices one should consider for everyday drinking rather than this. If you happen to like rosés, here's one to savor: quite dry, full-bodied, adequate aging for a nuance of lingering flavor.

On a special occasion you might want to sample a varietal such as a "big" Cabernet. Lost Hills Vineyards could have been mentioned in the claret section of everyday wines—it's priced there at less than four dollars for 1.5 liters. But here again there's something different in this winery's approach that makes its Cabernet and Chenin Blanc distinctive, worth setting aside for guests or a holiday. Compare it with Sebastiani's Mountain Cabernet, about $1.50 more for 1.5 liters; this has received the plaudits of many critics, but it's sometimes hard to find. Or compare both with Souverain's Zinfandel at still a little more in cost. You're still well under six dollars for a magnum, and you're now into a level of wine appreciation that you just can't get in French or Italian wines at this price. Perhaps the Rioja wines of Spain, the South African or the Australian cabernets come close. But the California products are known quantities and should be available with a little persistence.

At this price level you can also dip into the two other major red varietals: Pinot Noir and Petite Sirah (sometimes spelled Syrah). Sebastiani offers a rich Pinot Noir at the same magnum price as the Cabernet. Here indeed is evidence that California vintners may eventually produce a great one to match that vine in France. Winemasters, one of the brands of Guild, has both a Pinot Noir and Cabernet at a slightly higher price for 1.5 liters, but it has achieved something exceptional with its Petite Sirah at

ƒetzeR

1976
MENDOCINO
PETITE SYRAH
SPECIAL RESERVE
PRODUCED AND BOTTLED BY
ƒetzeR VineyaRÒs
REDWOOD VALLEY, CALIFORNIA
ALCOHOL 12.9% BY VOLUME

1976
PETITE SYRAH

This full-bodied and flavorful wine is made 100% from Petite Syrah grown in three carefully selected vineyards located in Mendocino County, California.

The grapes were delivered to our winery in mid-October 1976 at 23.5° Brix. After a long fermentation the wine was aged in small casks. It was bottled at our winery in the winter of 1978.

You will find this wine intensely fruity with a rich spicy character. This wine can be enjoyed now and will be greatly enhanced with further aging.

Leonard G. Fetzer

FETZER VINEYARDS

about six dollars. This grape has had only a few loyal supporters over the years among the major wineries, notably Concannon in Livermore Valley. Now the liquor stores have a separate section in their bins for Petite Sirah if they have one for the other reds. At its best, as it is with Winemasters, this varietal is full of rich aromas and deep in flavors.

Most of the wines mentioned in this chapter, with the exception of some dessert wines, come in the traditional magnum bottle. If you feel more comfortable serving guests out of that type of bottle instead of a squat jug, fine! As we will see, there are ways to make serving out of real jugs fun, too. Whatever your style, sooner or later you're going to have to sample the Sunday kind of jugs or some contemporary Lautrec will rightfully berate you as not being worthy of a Sunday wine: *you will never have any and you will never know what it is.*

It's also worth trying to develop your own evaluations of the wines you drink and a language suitable to describe those opinions to your friends. Enjoyment of a fine wine is a factor of both experience and concentration; and a conscious attempt to match tastes with words inevitably helps you concentrate. It's truly sad to see Sunday wines gulped down just because the drinker can easily afford them.

In this light, Lautrec's analogy of a peacock in the mouth isn't all that silly. James Thurber's famous cartoon underlines the absurdity of extravagant prose ("It's a naive wine without any breeding, but I think you'll be amused by its presumption"), but it's almost better to err on the side of extravagance than to go through life treating everything that goes in your mouth as nothing more than coal for the furnace.

We have already seen some of the key words used routinely to describe excellence in everyday wines: the whites are crisp, fresh, clean; the reds are mellow, hearty, rounded. At exceptional levels a wine has character, garnet hues, and a bouquet that fills the room. Fred Cherry has proposed a list of the most beautiful words to describe wine; can you top these: *intense, tender, supple, velvet, silken, seductive?* Reserve your best jug wines for special occasions, and save words like these for only the outstanding vintages!

5

House
Wines

*The wine of Arpad Haraszthy has a bouquet all
its own. It tickles and titillates the palate. It
gurgles as it slips down the alimentary canal. It
warms the cockles of the heart, and it burns the
sensitive lining of the stomach.*

— Ambrose Bierce, *Devil's Dictionary*

Wines served in carafes, in unlabeled bottles with a cork loosely tucked in
the top, or directly from a jug into the glass were, not too long ago, the
poor cousins of the restaurant wine trade. In many cases these "house
wines" did not receive the dignity of a place on the wine list. For a variety
of reasons the maker of the wine is still seldom mentioned in print, and
most waiters are unaware of what they are serving. Typically when one
asks a waiter what the white wine is he will answer, "It's a Chablis."

The growing awareness of wines among consumers is changing all this.
Restaurants are realizing that the choice of their establishment for lunch
especially hinges more and more on whether their everyday wines are up
to par.

In Bierce's day the reputation and consistency of any given wine
maker were not such as to inspire allegiance such as this. The gentleman
he mentions was, of course, the best-known California vineyard owner of
the late nineteenth century. Haraszthy almost single-handedly raised the
new-world vineyards to European standards by importing *Vitis vinifera*
cuttings from France. By a curious irony this transplant was to be the
salvation of French châteaux, too; when a plague known as the phylloxera
nearly wiped out the centuries-old vines in Bordeaux and Burgundy, the
hardier California root stock, on which Haraszthy's cuttings were grafted,
was imported by the French to replace the dying vines. To Mr. Bierce all

things were bitter, even the wine; but Haraszthy deserves better for his efforts. The Buena Vista Winery in Sonoma is his legacy, and another, newer winery currently bears his name.

The chances of a "bulk" wine going bad in transit from the winery to the restaurant or bar are today practically nil. Air and heat are wine's only enemies, and in Bierce's day storage conditions allowed both to do their damage. My father tells me of the hogsheads of wine resting in the cellar on the farm through the winter and spring; by the time the fierce summer sun had come over the Sacramento Valley and the level of the barrels was below half full, the wine had changed to another thing entirely. But today most wines are pasteurized and heavily refined of all "impurities" (on the pity of this, more later), and most wholesalers keep the product out of the direct rays of the sun and below 70°F. in the warehouse. You can safely leave a gallon (sorry, 3 liters) half full for a week or two without risking it going bad. In fact, the aeration a wine receives as the jug is slowly emptied is a form of instant aging. Opening a fine old bottle to "let it breathe" is merely a process of aeration, as is swirling the wine around your mouth and sucking it into your cheeks. Among other things, aging is the bringing of air into controlled contact with the liquid—slow oxidation. As a rule of thumb, a ten-degree increase in temperature doubles the chemical activity in a solution. So a bottle sitting in a store window is being oxidized much faster than if it were in the shade. And the chance of a wine going bad sitting almost *empty* in a *hot* kitchen is very good.

For these reasons I applaud the restaurants that pour their house wines in a conspicuous fashion directly from the jug into your carafe or glass. You know if you're getting the bottom of the jug, and you know if the jug is too warm. Most bars keep their jug wines in plain view; not so the restaurants. The best assurance you can have that the house wine will be what the vintner intended is a rapid turnover of jugs in the restaurant. In the case of white wines, which are refrigerated, the problem is minimal. But if a red house wine begins to taste "off"—send it back. Almost literally, a rejected house wine means nothing to the restaurateur.

THE MARKUP

The greatest profit item in a restaurant, it goes without saying, is not the food but the drinks. And the best markup for the restaurateur is not the cocktail but the house wine. The more elegant restaurants take the most advantage of this fact, since their by-the-glass prices were set quite high years ago when they poured wine from fifths. It's not unusual to pay two dollars for a glass of wine worth ten or fifteen cents. (Figure it out—a generous glass of six ounces is one-twentieth of a gallon or less, and a gallon can wholesale for less than $2.50 and still be a very good wine.) More common is to pay $1.00 or $1.25 for the same glass—still an excellent markup. In cities where wine drinking is yet something of a strange custom—and these aren't at all small cities—one is often poured only a few ounces for one's dollar because the restaurant has only thimble-size sherry glasses on hand, or chooses to have such on hand. My record for the smallest glass of wine for the steepest price is a Japanese restaurant in New York City, but the practice is widespread. Italian and French restaurants are the most realistic, in terms of the customer, and West is better than East. Hotels are the worst offenders, along with those restaurants that feel anything larger than a ping pong ball isn't delicate enough for a good place setting. But these are far too general admonitions.

What is one to do? In a strange restaurant or bar, look around for wine glasses, and, not seeing any, ask for one before ordering. A small carafe (usually one-half liter) is at least two and a half generous glasses and always a better buy than a glass for two people, or for one person intending to have a real taste of the wine. Frank Schoonmaker's characteristic riposte to a waiter who asked if he wanted a full bottle was, "I don't want an empty one." A full bottle—a fifth—and a full one-liter carafe *should* be about equal in price for the same quality of wine. The corked bottle always fetches more in expense-account restaurants, sometimes hideously more. A rule of thumb is that the lowest-priced wine on the wine list shouldn't be more than 20 percent higher than a liter of the house wine, and then, of course, the house wine is still a bargain if it's any of the ones you like at home.

Burger's Rule now comes into play: *It's never déclassé to ask for a wine list.* Ask for it before ordering cocktails: you and your party may surprise each other finding that most of you prefer wine to hard liquor anyway. Ask for the wine list before deciding on the house wine, even if you intend that all along. Ask the waiter what the house wine is—the wine maker or the label, not the type. Stephen Potter would approve of you if, after being told that the house wine is Emile's, you ask, "Chablis or Blanc Sec?" Ask for the wine list before ordering dessert: you and your party may be quite content with another good bottle of wine and some cheese. Finally, ask for the wine list at all nightclubs or other places where there is a minimum charge for entertainment, or a minimum number of drinks, or simply minimum service. Don't place an order for the perfunctory scotch or gin and tonic when you know it's going to be a minimal drink, the charge for which is for the entertainment, anyway. Order a good bottle of wine and sit back and relax, knowing that you will not be hounded for a second round. Yes, ask for a wine list whenever you can't make up your mind about anything: it's also a good stall.

Never feel sorry for a restaurateur who sells a lot of house wine: he's doing all right. Many of the big wine makers offer special containers to save the restaurateur even more money and time. Almadén has a dispenser that sits in a cardboard box and fills glasses like a water cooler. Wineries like Christian Brothers and Inglenook have special gallon jugs, or other larger sizes, which are sold only to bars and restaurants. The 4.9-gallon container—a demijohn of the size that bottled water comes in—is now common. I've mentioned that many wineries, such as San Antonio, have chosen the 4-liter container instead of the 3-liter, just for the economy of the restaurant trade. Wine is, in these superjugs, the best news for restaurants since the president stopped talking about two-martini lunches.

BRAND LOYALTY

Bar or restaurant owners who have little respect for the tastes of wine drinkers are constantly switching wine brands, especially their house wines. Many carry on this game of musical chairs in the delusion that they're experimenting to find the best or acceding to the wishes of their best customers. A typical conversation at the bar, two men waiting for a table:

"Hey, what's this wine?" (Mild surprise.)
"Growers—do you like it?" (Expecting approval.)
"Terrible stuff—why don't they get Cribari or Mondavi?" (With authority.)
"Hey, Joe (to the bartender), when're you going to switch to a decent jug wine?" (Now an expert.)

The general rule is no one praises the house wine—that shows lack of savoir faire. When the bartender or restaurateur hears this conversation over and over, he switches to another brand just to show everyone he's trying. Salesmen from the major brands are always waiting in the wings; in fact, they're usually dropping around to leave samples, and the restaurateur lets the same favorite customers try the samples. The corollary to the general rule is that all free samples taste better than anything anyone ever ordered.

One way that brand loyalty is established is through the practice, popularized by Almadén, of the wine maker printing free wine lists for the restaurant in return for supplying not only the house wine but almost everything else as well. The smaller ethnic restaurants—Chinese, Mexican, Japanese—are natural customers for this one-call-does-it-all arrangement. Sometimes it's the distributor who supplies the wine list—and perhaps the menu, too. His brands then make up most of the liquor purchased.

A better way to have some consistency in the wine list is for the owner of the establishment to make a decision after careful tasting and simply stick to his guns. A known quantity always appeals more than a grab bag—to customers who care about wine. In my experience, the better the restaurant, the more confidence it has in its house wine. I know several that have kept the same jugs in the well for more than ten years. If you can set your watch by certain trains, you can tune your taste buds by certain favorite eating places.

Yet the changes are so great from year to year that I hesitate to attempt a comprehensive listing of who serves what. Instead, on the following pages I've given a sample of what one can expect in a large Midwestern city—I've chosen the Midwest because this is the region where the wine boom is just around the corner. Chicago is a natural choice with its hundreds of restaurants of all types. From my sampling of about fifty popular restaurants, I found that about ten percent serve no house wine, and almost every nationality is represented with a jug wine or house wine of its country. California wines predominate, but the traditional loyalty to French and Italian wines is still quite strong. This is not at all intended as a guide to Chicago house wines, but just as a picture of what you can expect throughout this region.

In the East, imported wines are even more popular than in the Midwest, both in liquor stores and in restaurants. (See Appendix for some comparisons of Italian and French jug wines.) Yet the swing to California brands is unmistakable. I have sampled wines in New York City for more than twenty years; if my experience is typical at all, the big change didn't occur until 1969 or 1970 and has accelerated since, as all of the premium California wineries gained distribution in the Northeast. Rapid improvements in quality of domestic wines, including many Eastern ones, and rapid increases in prices of imports were the two big factors in this trend. Then came the switch to white wines; domestic brands have their real strength here, and they have the volume. In New York City and Washington, D.C. especially, French red wines are still considered the important reds, and the reputation of California jug reds has not yet caught up with their quality.

To capture some of the flavor of how certain restaurants prefer certain house wines in different parts of the country, I've appended a random sample of the places I've personally visited recently. This list, too, is highly subjective and may be somewhat out of date as you read this. But it's not intended as a guide, only a sampling. Northern California figures heavily in the list of restaurants because this is sort of a proving ground for the major wineries in the state. This region has the highest per capita consumption of wine in the country. Los Angeles accounts for the greatest volume of any American city with New York second. Washington, D.C. now has a per capita consumption of California wine second only to San Francisco.

Trying various house wines at bars and restaurants is an expensive but effective way to sample jug wines. There is no other place where you can get the feedback you'll get here—from other customers, from the owner, and sometimes from a salesman from a winery. ...

Rating Chicago on House Wines

Almadén
Jonathan Livingston Seafood
Great Gritzhes
Gejas
D. B. Kaplans Deli
French Kitchen (Chablis)

The Christian Brothers
Gaylord India

Franzia
Hachney's (Burgundy)
   at various locations

Foppiano
Courthouse

Gallo
Blackhawk, on Pearson (Burgundy)

Guild
Le Berdeaux (Chablis)

Geyser Peak
Otto's

Inglenook
Rusty Scupper
Magic Pan
Henrici's

Charles Krug (C. K. Mondavi)
Doros
Geno's Pizzeria
Como Inn
Maple Tree Inn

Louis Martini
Kon Tiki Ports

Paul Masson
French Kitchen (Burgundy)
Junk

Sebastiani
Blackhawk, on Pearson (Chablis)

Mirassou
Blackhawk, on Wabash (Chablis)

Souverain
Cape Cod Room, Drake Hotel

Summit
Gnauer's Oyster Bar

Taylor
Hachney's (Chablis)
   at various locations
Khyber Indian

Winemasters
French Kitchen (Rosé)

The fact that other fine California wines didn't show up in my sample is only the luck of the draw. Some restaurants, like the Bakery and Gene &

Georgetti's, serve a good list of California wines just in fifths, but at reasonable prices. The French influence is still quite strong; various French bulk wines were available at L'Auberge, Le Berdeaux (red), Blackhawk (on Wabash), Cafe at the Ritz, Farmer's Daughter, Le Festival, Left Bank, the Pump Room. Other national favorites were represented at Berghoff (Austrian), Greek Islands (guess), La Margarita (Mexican), Lutz (German), Lou Malnetti's (Italian). Two wines showed up which I believe are popular only in the Midwest: Glunz, at the Blackhawk (on Wabash) and the Pump Room, and Carbone, at the popular pizzerias, Uno's and Due's. A trend that is more popular in the East is evident here too— California jug wines bottled especially for one restaurant with their own label (Waterfront).

NEW YORK, DALLAS, DENVER, LOS ANGELES, SAN FRANCISCO . . .

The Almadéns, Fetzers, Sebastianis, Gallos, Colonys, and Inglenooks are represented all over the country, but dozens of other California brands are moving in on these front-runners. Giumarra recently advertised "Over 500 Fine Restaurants Have Recently Selected Giumarra as Their House Wine." For a winery that was almost anonymous a few years ago, this is impressive. Los Hermanos, the Beringer jug wine, is served in Victoria Stations across the land, as well as the TGIF chain and Stouffers. Some of its major Eastern accounts are Windows on the World and Mortimers in New York City, Manor in New Jersey, and the Chart Houses in Massachusetts and Connecticut. Wines like Cribari's Burgundy and Vino Bianco are enjoyed all the way across the country at places like Hose Company Number Six, in Pawtucket, Rhode Island, while the Tribuno Wines imported Luigi Pomponi Rosso and Bianco Romagna are shipped from Chicago, Illinois to New Orleans, Louisiana to be served at Commander's Palace. Pedroncelli not only serves the restaurants near its headquarters, such as Catelli's in Geyserville and House of Sonoma in Healdsburg, but also ships to the Northwest, to such places as Jake O'Shaughnessy's in Seattle. It's interesting that Pedroncelli is following the trend popularized by Fetzer and Robert Mondavi in avoiding the generic names "Burgundy" and "Chablis" in favor of simply "Red" and "White." Parducci also is served in Victoria Stations at various locations, at a hometown restaurant in Ukiah, the Palace, and at the unique Nut Tree in Vacaville. Barengo has limited distribution outside California, but is used as a house wine at some well-known places around the state: the Senator Hotel in Sacramento, the Sheraton-Newport in Newport Beach, and the Whale's Tail in Oxnard. JFJ Bronco is served in the Charlie Brown restaurants around the country; some typical locations in California are Anna's

Restaurant in Los Angeles and The Nest in Ranch Mirage. Guasti is extending its on-sale locations throughout California and into the Midwest, and it's the kind of wine that fits with Sizzler Steak Houses (Westwood), Lyons (Santa Rosa and Napa), or the more elegant Fior D'Italia (San Francisco) and The Pelican (Playa Del Rey). Guasti's varietals are priced at a level at which they're finding acceptance as house wines, too.

A winery always welcomes the recognition it's afforded when a restaurant that prides itself on its cuisine chooses that winery from the scores of excellent ones in the marketplace to provide the house jug. The winery receives the tacit approval of the restaurant owner, and his customers have the opportunity to use the house wine as a sort of "benchmark" of their own in experimenting with the wine list. Cresta Blanca, for example, is proud to be known as the winery of choice "by the glass" or "by the carafe" at The Saloon in Beverly Hills, the Forum Club in Inglewood, and Mario's in Palm Springs. In Westwood, a favorite dining establishment of entertainers, Matteo's, prefers Cribari. Delicato Vineyards is the choice at Beefeeders in Los Angeles. The Christian Brothers are teaching them how to quaff at the Tracton Restaurant in Los Angeles.

Where the bar predominates over the dining room, wines by-the-glass tend to become a matter of economics rather than careful choice. Wine is a compromise between stiffer drinks and mineral water for a growing number of people who frequent taverns, pubs, saloons, and other hangouts. It fulfills the purpose first enunciated by Aristophanes: "Quickly, bring me a beaker of wine so that I may wet my mind and say something clever." Or, more recently, the gloss by Frederick Exley: "Unlike some men, I have never drunk for boldness or charm or wit. I have used alcohol for precisely what it is—a depressant to check the mental exhilaration produced by extended sobriety." Given such proclivities, the bar owner thoughtfully selects a house wine that has some liveliness and color, but in the long run *staying power*. And at the right price. Several establishments I have known are worth mentioning for their success in meeting these requirements. In New York, Munk's in lower midtown Manhattan pours a good glass of Sebastiani; and Mulligan's in the Carnegie Hall area has a crisp, white wine made by Great Western and named simply Rhine Wine, one of the great bargains in the city. Around the corner, Eddie Condon's serves Soave Bolla (see Appendix), not a bad choice considering the international character of the jazz, the other house specialty. All of these establishments exhibit the essential characteristic of a good watering hole: some interest other than ethanol.

In Dallas, the Downtown Point is a good choice when the town seems to have picked up and gone for the evening. Here the ostensible interest is football talk, and Almadén is served from one of those cardboard dispensers. When it is called Alma*deen*, the picture is complete. Nearby Mariano's offers a combination of superb Mexican food at the bar or in booths, turn-of-the-century back-bar and furniture, a railroad train coursing endlessly overhead below a pressed-tin ceiling with Casablanca fans, and Inglenook Navalle Chablis.

Denver sports one of the most sensible bars in the country—Duffy's. The Third Avenue atmosphere works well for businessmen or Irish celebrators, the price is right ($1.95 for a half-liter carafe), and the wines are selected with care: Paul Masson Riesling and Sebastiani Cabernet!

The Irish bar in downtown Los Angeles is Casey's, serving Summit wines there and at their Westwood location—again at a truly house wine price and with the nonchalance that distinguishes the self-conscious imitation Irish bar from this, the real thing.

Frank's Italian Bar in San Francisco's North Beach pours Louis Martini reds and whites from the well, the Washington Square Bar & Grill trusts in Cresta Blanca and Sebastiani (white) and doesn't measure it out sparingly, and a dozen other, mainly Italian cantinas in this neighborhood stay loyally with brands one may never have heard of. The last holdout among the new high rises between the Financial District and North Beach, The Iron Pot has served Valley of the Moon red and white from its jugs for more than a dozen years. The thinking man's Irish bar, Harrington's, insists on Growers for the tastes of its clientele. As the birthplace of the California wine industry, it's worth surveying what goes on in the city's restaurants a little more thoroughly.

A Sampling of House Wines: San Francisco Bay Area:

C. K. Mondavi
Spenger's (Berkeley)
Cliff House (San Francisco)
Joe's Westlake (Daly City)

Cribari
Tadich Grill (San Francisco)
Candlestick Park
  (home of the
  San Francisco Giants and '49ers)

The Christian Brothers
The Spinnaker (Sausalito)
Zim's (San Francisco)

Emile's
Orsi's (San Francisco)
Paoli's (San Francisco)
St. Pierre (San Francisco)
Chez Leon (San Francisco)
Original Joe's
  (San Francisco, San Jose)
L'Auberge (Redwood City)
Deetjen's Big Sur Inn (Big Sur)
Le Camembert (Mill Valley)

Delicato Vineyards
Henry's Fashion (San Francisco)
McArthur Park (San Francisco)

Foppiano Vineyards

Alioto's No. 8 (San Francisco)

Mayes Oyster House
  (San Francisco)

North China (Berkeléy)

Mirabeau (Oakland)

Khyber Pass (Oakland)

Scotty Campbell's (Redwood City)

The Dock (Tiburon)

Wine Country (Healdsburg)

Louis Martini

Clift Hotel (San Francisco)

Anchor Cafe (San Francisco)

Engineer's Club (San Francisco)

The major clubs in the city—the Bohemian, the Family, the University, and so forth—choose their house wines as any restaurant would, with perhaps more concern about that elusive quality, staying power. Their members frequent the club on a more regular basis than the average person patronizes a favorite restaurant. What is surprising, therefore, is the great range of selections. The above listings make that point, too. The length of the restaurant list after any of the wineries shown is no indication of preference for the winery: all the major wineries and many of the smaller ones have dozens of on-sale accounts. The list just shows a little of the variety that is there for the restaurant-goer.

There is an institution in San Francisco that deserves special mention for wine buffs who like jug wine prices but prefer premium wine tastes. The London Wine Bar, in the Financial District, offers premium wines from all countries by the glass—at prices that one often pays for a glass from a jug. Depending on the price of the bottle, the glass price can run from $1.25 to $2.00 or more. And the selection changes at least once a week. In addition, a bottle of wine can be purchased at the off-sale price from the large selection in the basement, and then corked for yourself and your guests for $1.00 more. Again, the equivalent of most jug wine prices offered by the house. I have seen a few similar combinations of retail liquor store with bar and restaurant, in Carmel, Santa Barbara, and Los Angeles; but this one has an exceptional range and ambiance. I have also seen restaurants, mainly in the northern California area, which have reduced the markup on their premium wines to the level where they *almost* compete with jug wines. But this trend is not evident elsewhere. It is with great reluctance that restaurateurs give up the wine "profit center."

Years ago there were several California wine makers who relied completely on supplying house wines, often in specially made-up labels, to Eastern hotels and restaurants. As we have seen, many still do, but almost all of them have now promoted their own labels more strenuously. Yet I have seen these unusual names in East Coast cities, in stores and restaurants: Fior di California, Gambarelli & Davitto (San Francisco), Romano (Cucamonga), Opici Homemade wine (San Francisco), Aquino (Sonoma), Toscani Chenin Blanc (Manteca), Fortino (Gilroy), and Orsini (Elk Grove).

Once I discovered, in a Buffalo, New York restaurant, that the only California wine on the list had an unfamiliar label with Hayward, California as the location. I was never able to locate the winery, though I did my best—because the wine was quite a bargain. On another occasion I found myself in Leonia, New Jersey with time on my hands, so I naturally made a survey of the wine market. To my surprise I discovered there were no bars at all—but at least a half a dozen full-service liquor stores in the space of a few blocks, with a selection of California wines superior to anything I had seen in New York. Moral: the compensations of nature extend even to wines. There is now, and there always will be, enough individuality and mystery in everyday wines that even if an occasional one burns the sensitive lining of your stomach there will always be another to lift your spirit.

6

Touring the Jug Wine Country

The smack of California earth shall linger
on the palate of your grandson.
                                    —Robert Louis Stevenson

Three miles outside the sleepy farm town of Gilroy, California, at the beginning of the sun-withered foothills that tell the traveler he is leaving the San Francisco Bay Area, a board and batten shed in a cluster of apricot trees just off a county road bears the hand-painted sign, "Peter Giretti— Harry Giretti Bonded Winery." It is operated now as it was when it was founded by the Girettis' father in 1912: the floors are earthen, there is no telephone, and wine is sold only in 5-gallon demijohns and 25-gallon barrels. The existence of such a place would have to be imagined in a novel if it did not stand there before you in fact. It is the vision of the jug wine tourer.

Unfortunately, there are not many wineries like the Girettis'—at least as far as the 5- and 25-gallon containers go. Most wineries bottle their product in half gallons, and virtually all of them in fifths—or the new metric equivalents. Most have telephones. Most have concrete or wooden floors. Yet there are scores of small, family-type operations that retain the spirit projected by the Girettis, even if they have come a little farther into the twentieth century.

A recent issue of a regional magazine listed 130 wineries with an annual production capacity of less than 72,000 gallons. That may seem like a lot of wine, but it's dwarfed by any of the wineries mentioned thus far. At the lower limits, a winery would have to produce at least 2,000 gallons to be in business at all; even at this level the industry often refers to it as a hobby. When the winery starts to win prizes and attract high prices, the competitiors call it a "boutique."

A PROFILE OF THE LITTLE OLD WINE MAKER

Many of the wineries in the 130 "small" ones are big enough to find their way onto restaurant wine lists and to be distributed outside the state. They are certainly worth visiting, but they're not places to explore for bargains or for jugs: Alexander Valley Vineyards, Davis Bynum Winery, Hop Kiln Winery—in Healdsburg; Chateau St. Jean—in Kenwood; Hanzell Vineyards—in Sonoma; Gundlach-Bundschu Winery—in Vineburg; Chateau Montelena, Cuvaison, and Schramsberg Vineyards—in Calistoga; Burgess Cellars, Chateau Chevalier Winery, Conn Creek Vineyards, and Stony Hill Vineyards—in St. Helena; Cakebread Cellars, Caymus Vineyards, and Grgich Hills Cellar—in Rutherford; Clos du Val, Mayacamas Vineyards, Stags Leap Winery, and Trefethen Vineyards—in Napa; Gemello Winery-in Mountain View; Ridge Vineyards—in Cupertino; Martin Ray—in Saratoga; Bertero Winery—in Gilroy; Chalone Vineyard—in Soledad; and The Firestone Vineyard—in Los Olivos. These names should be familiar to anyone who has dabbled in wine. Many are large enough to advertise. Several have won awards here and abroad. Some are the product of successful businessmen who have embarked on a new career with wine: Stony Hill, Mayacamas, Firestone. Schramsberg made national news when then-President Nixon chose its champagne for state functions. I've mentioned Bertero previously: the price level and quality of these wines might be considered the starting point for the rest. Yet, even though the bargains aren't here, among these wineries are the more interesting locales and buildings that make a visit to them well worthwhile.

I picked grapes on the site of the present Hop Kiln Winery before the plans for making it a commercial enterprise had jelled. An old stone hop kiln, built in 1905 and now a state historical monument, was the focus of the owner's dream. Having seen the condition it was in ten years ago, I shudder at the persistence that was necessary to bring it to its present finished state. But the labor of love resulted at least in this: at the 1978 Los Angeles County Fair, Hop Kiln carried off a Gold Medal for its Zinfandel and a Silver Medal for what it called, quite justifiably, Sweetwater Springs A Thousand Flowers. Like most of the wineries mentioned here, it's open for tastings on weekends and by appointment on weekdays, with room for picnicking on the grounds near the vines. The ambience of Hop Kiln, including its labels, is typical of a field of business very untypical in our day.

At least by California's standards, there is history here as well. The Alexander Valley Vineyards is graced with a Victorian mansion and estate built in Gold Rush days. Chateau Chevalier Winery in St. Helena is the picture of the old-world château: a stone castle built in 1873–1891, with a spiral, wrought-iron staircase climbing up the center from basement to

SAN ANTONIO WINERY
Private Stock

ALCOHOL 18% BY VOLUME

CALIFORNIA
SHERRY
Golden amber with a distinctive nut-like flavor.

SouveRain
NORTH COAST
CHARDONNAY

produced & bottled at the winery by Souverain Cooperville Co Alcohol 13% by volume

SOLE AGENTS

BOTTLED IN CALIFORNIA

Famiglia
CRIBARI
MELLO BURGUNDY

HISTORIC CULTURAL MONUMENT NO. 42

Family Owned and Operated since 1917
SAN ANTONIO®

CALIFORNIA
VELVET VIN ROSÉ
A Premium Select Wine

MADE AND BOTTLED BY THE OLDEST OPERATING WINERY IN THE CITY OF LOS ANGELES
SAN ANTONIO WINERY, LOS ANGELES, CAL.

TWELVE PERCENT ALCOHOL BY VOLUME

Emile's
PRIVATE STOCK

CALIFORNIA
CHABLIS

In 1925 on fifteen fertile acres, Emilio Guglielmo's first harvest was nurtured to perfection. For three generations the Guglielmo family has celebrated this ritual and shared the finest wines with family and friends. This dedication to produce and share fine wines has made our family owned and operated winery more than a business — a way of life.

Emilio Guglielmo

ALCOHOL 12% BY VOLUME
PRODUCED & BOTTLED IN SANTA CLARA VALLEY, MORGAN HILL, CA. BY
EMILIO GUGLIELMO WINERY

GUILD · VINO DA
TAVOLA
RED
CALIFORNIA TABLE WINE

MADE AND BOTTLED BY GUILD WINE PRES LODI CALIF. ALC. 12% BY VOL

Unlike French labels, California's are as varied as the architecture of California's wineries.

second story. The Boeger Winery in Placerville boasts a wine cellar constructed in 1872 and listed in the *National Register of Historic Places.* Robert Louis Stevenson describes a visit to the Schramsberg Vineyards more than a century ago in *Silverado Squatters.* Unfortunately, none of the wines of that era survive for the grandsons of his contemporaries to sample today. Other wineries have undergone a sea change since their founding in the middle of the last century: Gundlach-Bundschu is a revival, by descendants of the original owner of the winery founded in 1858, and a grandson of the founder of V. Sattui Winery, which flourished in San Francisco's Mission District before the turn of the century and after, has reopened it in St. Helena.

Except for an extra hundred years or so of history, touring these wineries isn't much different from sampling those in the Finger Lakes region of New York or along the Hudson. Each offers a good view of what it's like to make wine, in relatively small quantities, an opportunity to talk with the actual owners and operators, and a chance to sample some of the local wine. None of this is peculiar to the *jug wine* aficionado; but as the wineries become smaller and the wines less pretentious, and more like jugs, more of the flavor of the wine-making process comes from a tour. The Christian Brothers winery in St. Helena is surely one of the most beautiful anywhere, including France, but a tour of it resembles an official state visit to a Ford assembly line by foreign dignitaries. Perhaps one such tour is educational; but I much prefer a casual conversation without the education.

The best way to go wine touring, with a jug in mind somewhere along the way, is to carve out a *region* for exploration rather than to aim for an individual winery. First of all, the single-destination winery may not live up to its name or description in the guide books. It may be closed—or chary with wine samples on a given day. Secondly, the point of a tour is really the picnic to follow—and you never know where the best place is to spread your blanket until you arrive on the scene and test a few sites.

TEN WEST COAST WINE TOURING AREAS

1. Portland-Seattle-Vancouver: The Pacific Northwest is a coming wine area, in spite of this latitude. As you might expect, whites are most suited to the climate, though some attempts have produced nicely balanced reds. Many brands from the Victoria and Portland areas, in particular, are making their way to California wine shops—proof enough that there is something going on here. Jugs haven't made their appearance here to the extent they have in California, but the local wines are often offered at everyday prices. This isn't a well-unified area, for geographical reasons, and may in the future be defined into many smaller units. But it's no longer de rigueur to ignore this corridor. Check chamber of commerce information for up-to-date availabilites of tours and tastings. Best bet: flinty-dry whites and berry-flavored wines.

2. *Napa-Sonoma-Mendocino:* Grapes may have been planted first in the southern part of the state, but this is where California made wine history. It's a big region, probably best referred to as North Coastal, but wineries throughout it are starting to give themselves appellations of location that are quite specific, such as Sonoma or Napa Valley. These are names that mean something on a label, because for all practical purposes virtually all the grapes used in these wines must come from the immediate vicinity. Two small wineries in Humboldt County might be included: Willow Creek Vineyards in McKinleyville and Wittwer Winery in Eureka. Further south and inland on U.S. 101 are a cluster of Mendocino County wineries, big and small: The major ones are Cresta Blanca and Parducci in Ukiah (and an ultramodern tasting room of Weibel); Fetzer in Hopland; Pedroncelli in Geyserville; Italian Swiss Colony·in Asti and Foppiano and Simi in Healdsburg. The small ones, not already mentioned in this chapter, are Edmeades, Husch, and Navarro Vineyards in Philo; Milano Winery in

California Chablis   Alcohol 12% By Volume
Made and Bottled by J.A.F. Vineyards, Geyserville, California

Hopland; Bandiera Wines, Pastori Winery, and Giuseppe Mazzoni, all in Cloverdale and all old-style family operations, the latter two going back to the 1910s; Trentadue and Vina Vista in Geyserville; Dry Creek, Field Stone, Johnson's Alexander Valley Wines, Lambert Bridge, Mill Creek Vineyards, A. Rafanelli, and Sotoyome Winery—all in Healdsburg; Mark West Vineyards in Forestville. In Windsor is the modern Sonoma Vineyards and the smaller Landmark Vineyards. Martini and Prati Wines in Santa Rosa is the first stop on the U.S. 101 route. Grand Cru Vineyards in Glen Ellen, Hacienda Wine Cellars and ZD Wines in Sonoma are some of the smaller ones further south, clustered around the major winery of Sonoma: Sebastiani, where a lovely motto is carved into an oak cask in Italian: "When one glass invites another, the wine is good." At Hacienda,

one can rent a bin to store one's purchases, sort of a private tasting room. Just over the hills in Napa Valley are many smaller wineries: Stonegate in Calistoga; Pope Valley Winery, Burgess Cellars, Robert Keenan Winery, Nichelini, Raymond Vineyard and Cellar, Round Hill Cellars, Smith-Madrone, and Yverdon—all in St. Helena in the company of Hans Kornell, Christian Brothers, Freemark Abbey, Inglenook, Beringer, Sutter Home, Louis Martini, and C. K. Mondavi. In Rutherford, where Beaulieu and Heitz have their home, are the smaller wineries of Cassayre-Forni Cellars, Caymus, and Rutherford Vintners. Robert Mondavi's modern mission-style winery is a standout along the highway further down at Oakville; here, too, the century-old Villa Mt. Eden Winery is again operating. Near Napa are Alatera Vineyards, Tulocay Winery, and Wooden Valley Winery, all quite small.

Perhaps the three finest wine-tasting rooms in the world are located in this region within a short drive of each other, though only one offers what might be called an *everyday* wine. Souverain's chateaulike winery and restaurant sit proudly at the head of Alexander Valley on U.S. 101; visitors can taste, dine elegantly, or picnic nearby. Domaine Chandon in Yountville is a French outpost for the production of sparkling wines on California soil (don't call it "champagne" here); and it is also one of the finest French restaurants in northern California. And "the winery of the twenty-first century" basks in the sun at the head of the valley, its white-washed, rectangular buildings jutting up on a knoll like a village on the Adriatic. This is Sterling—something of an anomoly in the valley because it was founded by Englishmen, though now part of the Coca Cola stable of wineries. It's one of the few wineries I know of that one has to pay to visit: a charge for use of the overhead tram that takes one from the parking lot to the villa on the hill. Yet even this fee is not bothersome because it is refunded against any purchase of wine and thus visitors are narrowed down to those who are serious. The English influence extends from the name, to the civility of the tour, to the elegant furnishings of a long dining room reserved for private parties. The winery itself seems to be operated by remote control; visitors can browse through the crushing area, among the fermentation tanks, and along rows of small Limousin oak aging barrels—as if these were the stacks of a library. There are no guides with memorized talks, no guards to keep one back: strategically placed, illus-trated signs explain the entire wine-making process in detail and in good humor, allowing the browser to take in as little or as much as he chooses. Emerging from the top of the last aging room, one enters a broad court-yard overlooking the length of the valley. Picnic tables invite families to settle under the trees for lunch. Further up the hillside is the magnificent tasting room, and here another nod to graciousness: the tourers seat themselves at tables on a patio or indoors and waiters or waitresses bring wines to the table for tasting. Among these, in all this elegance, are Sterling's jugs (see chapter 4). Orders placed in the shop below are relayed to the storage area at the bottom of the tram, so that when one alights from the gondola his bottles or cases are waiting to load into the car. Whether this is to your taste or not, you must admit it extends the gamut of tours a long way from the brothers Giretti.

3. *San Francisco Bay Area:* Once the center of the Northern California wine trade, San Francisco is now without a winery, but a few surround the bay. In San Rafael the Grand Pacific Vineyard Co. offers daily tastings, as do two stores within blocks of each other in Berkeley: Oak Barrel Winery and Wine and the People. One might expect this type of store in Berkeley, combining winery, tasting room, and a sales room for everything one

needs to make wine at home. Wine and the People makes a substantial Cabernet from grape concentrate, as if to demonstrate to home wine makers around the country that the lack of vineyards in their vicinity shouldn't stop them from attempting a noble vintage. In nearby Emeryville are two nationally known wineries of the boutique type: J. W. Morris Port Works and Veedercrest Vineyards. The latter has grown from a home-type operation in Berkeley and will eventually move to Napa Valley. The Conrad Viano Winery in Martinez also offers daily tastings—rare for most of the small wineries listed here unless one calls ahead. Across the

CRESTA BLANCA®

SINCE 1882

Mendocino
Zinfandel

PRODUCED AND BOTTLED BY
CRESTA BLANCA WINERY • SAN FRANCISCO, CALIFORNIA B.W.C.4416
——— ALCOHOL 12% BY VOLUME ———

river is the small Diablo Vista Winery in Benecia—once the state's capital. To the south are the Obester Winery in Half Moon Bay and Richard Carey Winery in San Leandro. Altogether, not a wide selection, but all within easy distance of San Francisco.

4. Livermore Valley: The most overlooked wine area in northern California is nestled in a corridor just beyond the East Bay hills and above the Central Valley in elevation and climate. Mission San Jose, a picturesque village in danger of being swallowed up by urban sprawl, is at the entrance to this region and is the home of the Weibel Champagne Winery, named for its leading product. The tasting rooms here and at world-famous Wente and Concannon in Livermore are homey and well run. Villa Armando in nearby Pleasanton also offers a garden area where sandwiches are served and a continental restaurant where wines available only at the winery are on the list. Stony Ridge Winery is the new name for a rustic, red-brick winery in Pleasanton that was winning medals at the Chicago World's Fair before the turn of the century. It, too, is open daily for tours, tasting, and picnicking. Unique among the wine regions of California, all of the wineries here hearken back to the 1800s and seem pleasantly untouched by time today.

5. *North Central Valley:* The interior valleys of California can't be lumped together indiscriminately, for the wineries directly east of the Bay

SERVE COLD

Rhinewine
California White Wine

CELLARED AND BOTTLED BY
JFJ Winery
CERES, CALIFORNIA ⚭ ALCOHOL 11½% BY VOLUME

Area speak lovingly of the breezes from the Delta on one side and the influence of the snow-capped Sierra on the other. In any event, the world's largest winery is located here, Gallo, and the sizable operations of Franzia, JFJ, Bronco, and Delicato in close proximity indicate something is going on. Franzia and Delicato (the family name is Indelicato, by the way) have large tasting rooms and are havens for travelers up and down U.S. 101 and to and from Yosemite. East-Side Winery and Winemasters are the places to stop in Lodi. Further north, in Elk Grove, Gibson awaits you. And there are several smaller wineries hereabouts, open for tastings by appointment: Sequoia Cellars in Woodland, Paolo Alvera in West Sacramento, and Borra's Cellar in Lodi. The Bella Napoli Winery in Manteca sells a "farmer's wine" in jugs.

Though Gallo is open only for VIP tours—vintners and enologists from around the world come to see how the brothers do it—it's deserving of special attention as the acknowledged leader of the jug wine movement. Critics come expecting the inevitable—to be impressed by size. There is that, of course: a single warehouse covering twenty-five acres with a railroad siding inside, and the largest glass-making factory west of the Mississippi. But visitors go away impressed more by the systematic application of quality control—and by a big surprise in store for the wine world a few years from now. We will come to this in a minute.

What is most remarkable in all this is that the Gallo story of quality is only now making an impact with the broad public. Few realize that Ernest and Julio launched a new era in grape planting in 1968 by offering unprecedented long-term contracts to growers of certain varietal grapes. The condition of these 10- and 15-year guarantees was that the grapes would be watched carefully to meet Gallo standards. The result has been a systematic planting of the best varietals for each growing area; in the recent past speculators put in Cabernet and Chardonnay willy-nilly, and reaped the harvest, for even great varietals can fail in the wrong soil. Few realize either that Gallo has a large investment in a Napa Valley co-op to supply the grapes needed for their premium wines. Almost a third of all the grapes grown in the North Coast counties go to Gallo—and 40 percent of all the Chenin Blanc crushed in the state!

A tour of their labs underlines one of the beauties of size: scientific capability equal to that of any university enology department in the world, with the possible exception of the University of California at Davis. Indeed, Gallo "graduates" have gone on to top positions at such wineries as Freemark Abbey, Cuvaison, Sebastiani, Souverain, Joseph Phelps, Chateau Montelena, Beaulieu, Paul Masson, Beringer, Franzia, The Monterey Vineyard, and San Martin. At the various sampling rooms in the Gallo labs, Ernest and Julio stop in after work every day to make a personal check of that day's production—by tasting it! The brothers delegate authority—for each of their wine categories a wine maker has the complete say-so of an independent vintner—but they also totally enmesh themselves in the details of all phases of their operations.

Now, the big surprise: Next to the Gallo neoclassical administration building is a large mound flanked by a man-made lake. In an underground cellar here of dramatic proportions, Yugoslavian craftsmen are putting together an array of small oak barrels that will age the next generation of Gallo premium wines. Some are already in the casks. When this winery within a winery is complete, and the varietals have reached their time in wood, there is going to be some excitement in the industry. The lake, by the way, is not there simply to provide the habitat for the Gallos' prized wildlife: it's to cool the new cellar with northern breezes.

Across the river in downtown Modesto is a welcoming sign for drivers on old U.S. 99: "Water, Weather, Contentment, Health." They might well have added, "Wine."

San Martin

1 9 7 7

California

CHABLIS

WHITE TABLE WINE

Produced and bottled by San Martin Winery   San Martin, California
Alcohol 12% by volume

TASTE ASSURANCE

We believe grapes of superior quality are produced only in specific geographic regions where the combination of sun, soil, and water are ideal for that particular grape variety. We will label each product with the content of each grape type and its origin, as your assurance of our commitment to this principle of quality.
CONTENTS: 42.4% French Colombard (San Joaquin County); 22.6% French Colombard (San Luis Obispo County); 12.7% French Colombard (Santa Clara County); 8.8% Pinot Blanc (Monterey County); 5.7% Emerald Riesling (Santa Clara County); 4.3% Pinot Blanc (Santa Clara County); 3.5% Johannisberg Riesling (Monterey County).

The San Martin COMMITMENT

We believe that grape varieties produce better quality and specific varietal character if they are grown in certain geographic regions. These geographic places, through a combination of climate, soil and water, treat grape varieties differently. The French for two centuries have known that the Cabernet Sauvignon is the master grape of Bordeaux, Pinot Noir of Burgundy and Chenin Blanc of The Loire.

Our varietal grapes are all from specific regions in California. We feel that they are worthy wines because their tastes represent the character of their geography; a meeting of the correct varietal grape with its most positive place for growth—in nature.

It will be our policy to label each product with:

—the Varietal grapes in each wine
—the percentage Varietal grape in each wine
—the geographic origin of each Varietal

We believe that place of origin is important in making fine wines. Our commitment to quality is based on this principle.

6. *The Gold Country:* A special pocket of climate blesses the Shenandoah Valley in the foothills where Captain John Sutter made his strike, and who knows if grapevines may not eventually pull more out of the soil than the miners did?

At the Placerville nexus of historic Route 49 are the Boeger and Sierra Vista Wineries; going south are Eldorado Vineyards in Camino and in Plymouth Consumnes River Vineyards, Monteviña, Shenandoah Vineyards, and d'Agostini. The latter is set against a hillside with storage cellars carved into it. Some of the barrels came around the Horn with the '49ers and are still in use.

Further along are the Amador Winery in Amador City, which produces Gold Nugget brands, Stone Ridge in Sutter Creek, and the Argonaut Winery in Ione. A tribute to the grape-growing potential of this region is the Silver Medal for a 1976 Amador County Zinfandel at the Los Angeles County Fair—made by Napa Wine Cellars of Oakville in Napa Valley!

The delightful hamlets of Murphys and Columbia contain, respectively, Chispa Cellars (in the basement of an 1856 building) and Yankee Hill Winery.

7. *Peninsula-Salinas Valley:* The big names here are Almadén and Paul Masson, the latter with tasting rooms in Saratoga and not at the winery. Many beer companies now sponsor distance races, but Masson is the only

winery I know that puts on a marathon (the Champagne Marathon). It also promotes local cultural events with concerts and even chess tournaments at the winery.

Starting on the San Francisco Peninsula and going south you could stop in for samples at such wineries as Woodside Vineyards and Sherrill Cellars in Woodside; Page Mill Winery in Los Altos Hills; Gemello and Sommelier in Mountain View; La Purisima in Sunnyvale; the prestigious Ridge Vineyards in Cupertino; Congress Springs, Mount Eden, and Martin Ray in Saratoga (the latter not to be confused with San Martin further down in San Martin on U.S. 101); David Bruce in Los Gatos; Ahlgren in Boulder Creek; Felton-Empire (formerly Hallcrest) in Felton; Frick, Roudon-Smith, Santa Cruz Mountain, and Sunrise—all in Santo Cruz; Bargetto's and Nicasio in Soquel. Inland on the route to Salinas are Richert & Sons, Sycamore Creek, and Pedrizetti in Morgan Hill, and several in Gilroy: Bertero, Fortino, Hecker Pass, Kirigin, Thomas Kruse, Live Oaks, and Rapazzini. After a side trip to Hollister and the wineries of Enz, Calera, and Cygnet, you can then turn to the coast for Monterey Peninsula Winery, Monterey, and Durney Vineyard, Carmel Valley. Further down U.S. 101 you'll come across Taylor and, in Soledad, Chalone. This is the region that is currently making great strides vis-à-vis its North Coastal region competitors, and it's predicted—or feared—that some day grapes may supplant artichokes and lettuce as the big cash crops here.

8. *South Central Valley:* Quite different in character from the major wineries further north, the operations from Fresno to Bakersfield have also been historically conditioned. Petri and Giumarra and DiGiorgio (Bear Mountain) once made wine anonymously for eastern buyers, and to a great extent still do. But the development of new hybrids to produce varietal grapes in the hot, irrigated vineyards of the interior valleys has been an important spur to new levels of quality throughout this region. Cribari in Fresno is the largest California winery open to the public, and its tasting rooms are quite popular. Nearby are A. Nonini Winery, Barengo in Acampo, and Farnesi in Sanger. The Papagni Vineyards further north at Madera and the Perelli-Minetti Winery in Delano are further evidence of the modern, controlled environments in wineries and skillful viticulture that are bringing more and more honors to a once-neglected growing region. The Setrakian Winery at Yettem not only ships many of its grapes north for crushing by smaller wineries, but brings North Coastal varietals south to make its premium white wines. And, in addition to the tours and samplings available at the wineries, tasting rooms are provided by several of these wineries in other parts of the state. Barengo, for example, maintains popular tasting centers at Farmer's Market in Los Angeles and in Red Bluff just off Interstate 5.

9. Santa Maria-Santa Barbara: No large wineries here, but a string of historic locations for tasting and picnicking from Paso Robles south on U.S. 101 to San Louis Obispo and Santa Barbara—an easy day's tour. Hoffman Mountain Ranch Vineyards has its tasting room in Paso Robles. In nearby Templeton are Las Tablas Winery and York Mountain Winery, both open daily. In Santa Maria is Rancho Sisquoc Winery, and in the mountains beyond are Los Alamos Winery, The Firestone Vineyard at Los Olivos, and Santa Ynez Valley Winery. The Firestone winery and tasting room is a good example of architectural refinement to match the spirit of today's wines. The Santa Barbara Winery is near the center of town and also offers daily tastings.

10. Los Angeles Area South: Occasionally a sprawling city will engulf an old winery, and the winery will choose to remain as factories and office buildings grow up around it. Such is the case with Gemello, in Mountain View, and in a more dramatic way with San Antonio Winery in Los Angeles. A short drive from the downtown area, this family-owned and operated establishment is the Italian winery one pictures in reading guide books and travel brochures: an arbor along the parking lot for picnicking, old winepresses, a wine museum of odd bottles and corkscrews, a cheese shop, and an informal restaurant that dissolves into the aging tanks of the winery itself. The tang of fermenting wine wafts over the trellised ceilings as hearty Italian lunches and snacks are served throughout the afternoon. Tours are informal and the Riboli family dispenses samples in the tasting room personally and generously. Factotum for the winery is Wolfgang Schoeppler, who one day may be in Disneyland or at the Madonna Inn servicing the winery's restaurant accounts, and the next day leading a tour through the aging rooms. San Antonio has nine other outlets in the Los Angeles area—a unique merchandising plan that keeps prices reasonable for jug and premium wines alike.

The J. Filippi Vintage Company employs a similar method of distribution—but also offers tastings at seven locations south of the Los Angeles area. Its jug wines include the varietals Chenin Blanc and Grenache Rosé.

Further south and inland are the Mount Palomar Winery in Temecula and the Ferrara Winery and San Pasqual Vineyards in Escondido. Wine buffs familiar with this area have every reason to venture across the border into Mexico and Baja California to sample some of the surprising wines now being made in these warmer climes. Santo Tomas Winery, for one, is attracting the attention of oenophiles for the quality it is achieving in the North Coastal style—it has as its wine maker the former headman at Beaulieu.

Wine touring is not the same as wine tasting. The usually small amounts of any one wine one samples aren't enough to tell very much, and

Great Western ®

ESTABLISHED 1860

PREMIUM NEW YORK STATE

Rhine Wine

Mellow white table wine
with a fragrant bouquet.

PRODUCED AND BOTTLED BY PLEASANT VALLEY WINE COMPANY
ALCOHOL 12% BY VOLUME   HAMMONDSPORT, N.Y. 14840

Great Western ®
NEW YORK STATE
PREMIUM WINES

This is one of many premium
New York State wines proudly
bearing the Great Western label:
a wide selection of red, white, and
pink table wines, both generic and
varietal; Solera Sherries and Ports;
vermouths; and America's most
honored Champagnes. Each
represents over a century of
wine-making tradition. Founded in
1860, ours was the first of the
Finger Lakes Wineries. And our
original Hammondsport wine cellars
still welcome visitors all year long.

the wines are usually presented at a counter in a crowd of tourers (sometimes in a plastic cup)—hardly a happy environment for wine enjoyment. One should come prepared to buy a bottle or two, not because it's any cheaper at the winery (in California it's more expensive with the advent of the discount wine store). You should take a good bottle home and sample it at a propitious time, with the memory of the winery and its people still in your mind. No, the tour of the winery and the atmosphere of the place are what make a trip to the wine country enjoyable. There are differences between even the most modern wineries, even though wine making is a simple process. You will learn that process most readily on a tour, especially in the autumn when grapes are coming in from the fields to be crushed. You will see the fermenting tanks, where the crushed grapes *could* turn into wine all by themselves from the wild yeasts on the skins; but in large containers there's too much natural yeast for a controlled fermentation, and besides the wine master prefers to use a cultured yeast of known quality. Therefore the crushed grapes are sulphured, and yeasts are put back in. When the fermentation has quieted, after a week or so, the purple or golden liquid is transferred to holding tanks or to aging containers—stainless steel, redwood, and for many premium types small Yugoslav or French oak barrels. (Larger oak barrels may soon be a thing of the past, the way the forests have been thinned to accommodate the vintners.) Is oak-aging a necessity? For the bigger wines, like the Cabernets and Chardonnays, the aroma of oak adds agreeable complexity to the "nose," the body, and the aftertaste. After that, it depends on the vintner's style. I've mentioned that Parducci has experimented with its '73 Cabernets by aging some in wood and a smaller quantity in stainless steel. John Parducci reasons: "People want to taste grapes, not barrels. The ancient Romans and Greeks never used wood to age wine, only clay amphora. Then someone invented barrels and since then we've all developed a taste for wood. Now that Americans understand wines, perhaps it's time they learned the true taste of wine." Fred Cherry and a group of guests tasted the '73 both ways, and found the "stainless steel" Cabernet a more drinkable wine. The wood-aged had lost its fruitiness, was astringent, and had a heavier bouquet. Barrel-aging is supposed to mature a wine sooner, because air is allowed to come in contact at a regulated rate with the wine in its formative stages. As the wine picks up tannin and other miniscule substances from the sides of the barrels, it falls to the bottom, initiating a cycle of circulation that is also helpful in maturing the wine. Finally, air enters the wood in controlled amounts, producing the gradual oxidation that is the essence of aging. Given all these facts, why does Parducci's stainless-steel-aging seem to produce a more pleasant wine? Only time will tell: drinkability and fruitiness are hardly the only measures. No doubt the tannin that was extracted from the walls of the barrels contributed to the

BROTHERHOOD'S 1979 TOUR SCHEDULE
SATURDAY & SUNDAY

FEB. 10 — NOV. 25   10 A.M. to 4 P.M.
Sunday — July & August Closing Extended 'till 5 P.M.

MONDAY thru FRIDAY

APRIL 30 — JUNE 22   12 noon to 3 P.M.
JUNE 25 — AUG. 31   10 A.M. to 4 P.M.
SEPT. 4 — NOV. 9   12 noon to 3 P.M.

Parking: Cars $1.50

Special fees for buses,
reservations required.

SPECIAL HOLIDAY TOURS 1979
From 10 A.M. to 4 P.M.

Lincoln's Birthday	Monday	Feb. 12
Washington's Birthday	Monday	Feb. 19
°Easter Season	Monday thru	Apr. 9-12
	Thursday	
	Monday thru	Apr. 16-20
	Friday	
Memorial Day	Monday	May 28
Independence Day	Wednesday	July 4
Labor Day	Monday	Sept. 3
Yom Kippur	Monday	Oct. 1
Columbus Day	Monday	Oct. 8
Thanksgiving	Friday thru	Nov. 23, 24, 25
Weekend	Sunday	

Closed: Thanksgiving, Christmas, New Year's, °Good Friday, °Easter Sunday

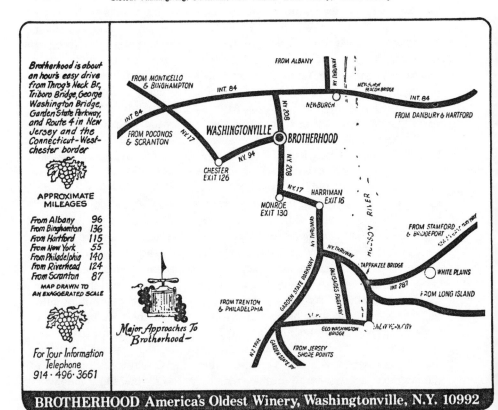

Brotherhood is about an hour's easy drive from Throg's Neck Br., Triboro Bridge, George Washington Bridge, Garden State Parkway, and Route 4 in New Jersey and the Connecticut-Westchester border

APPROXIMATE MILEAGES

From Albany   96
From Binghamton   136
From Hartford   115
From New York   55
From Philadelphia   140
From Riverhead   124
From Scranton   87

MAP DRAWN TO AN EXAGGERATED SCALE

For Tour Information Telephone 914-496-3661

Major Approaches To Brotherhood—

BROTHERHOOD America's Oldest Winery, Washingtonville, N.Y. 10992

astringency the tasters mentioned. In chapter 8 we'll see other experiments that are more appropriate to jug wines.

The process of making champagne, either the bulk (Charmat) way or by a second fermentation in the bottle, is also best understood after seeing it done. André Simon's loving book, *The History of Champagne,* captures the essence of what the bubbly is all about and reassures us there is no magic in any one method or style of making it. Long before Dom Perignon's time there were wines being made in the Champagne district that showed a little spritz or *frisson,* which, according to an account of 1588, "is why kings and princes often make it their favorite tipple."

Though wine touring and tippling is most inviting in California, with

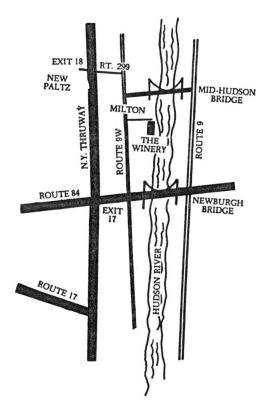

The Royal Winery is easily reached from all points. Follow route 9W to Milton, at the blinker light turn East (toward the river) and follow the signs. Open Sunday and every day except Saturday and Jewish Holidays. Tours May 1 to Dec. 31. 10 AM - 5 PM.

The Hudson Valley Wine Company is just north of The Royal Winery on N.Y. Route 9W.

its hundreds of wineries, the Easterner is not without resources on his home ground. In the Chautauqua region between Westfield and Niagara Falls, New York are several wineries open for inspection, concentrating on native grape types. (Native American Catawbas and Concords have traditionally been described as having a "foxy" taste. Considering the current use of that word, this may be all to the good; but no one really knows what a fox tastes like. Let's just say they have a pronounced flavor no matter what the wine type.) Another major region in New York, Finger Lakes, is producing more and more *Vitis vinifera* types every year. Wineries such as Taylor's Great Western and Widmer are located at Hammondsport, Geneva, Canandaigua, Naples, and Conesus. Within an hour's drive of New York City is the most interesting touring region in the East: Hudson Valley. There are many "boutique" operations similar to those in Napa Valley, but also a depth of history that goes beyond anything in California. The Brotherhood, Royal Wine Corporation, and High Tor vineyards are the major attractions, and tasting has been raised to a fine art at the Hudson Valley Wine Company, where banquets can be arranged at the Manor House. The Benmarl Vineyard here is making an interesting transition from the use of native grapes to specialization in the French and California varietals—a good place to find out which of them you prefer.

The success of a wine tour depends on ample time to browse, see at least one winery thoroughly, and visit three or so. An overnight stay is best: there's nothing quite like lodging in one of the old hotels on the town square in Sonoma and walking to the Hacienda Winery, Buena Vista, or Sebastiani, or staying in one of the towns on the trail of the '49ers. Jug wines never fail in the outdoors, on picnics or hikes. And you also want to spend some time visiting the local cantinas, mindful of Samuel Johnson's advice, "There is nothing which has yet been contrived by man, by which so much happiness is produced, as by a good tavern or inn."

7

Jug Wines
in the Kitchen

*The environment counts for much in the presentation
of a wine. The glasses should be thin, colourless, and
transparent. The wine will lend them a more glorious
colour than any hue the glass-founder can give them.
The Greeks of the classical age knew the perfect wine-
glass shape. Had they not modelled their cups from
Helen's divine breast?*

—H. Warner Allen, *The Romance of Wine*

Let's not speak of a cellar for jug wines. The kitchen will do. And there the
wine will also more likely be a part of the general gastronomy of the
household.

Wines can be used in more ways than sipping, quaffing, gurgling, and
they can be used in *cooking* in more ways than a ceremonial slug in the
coq au vin. I've mentioned that almost any meat improves with marinad-
ing; but this is merely a tenderizing process. The *flavor* of wine can also be
imparted to dishes, and the beauty of jug wines is that you can afford to
experiment with them wherever water is called for in a recipe. Likewise
the color of wine can add a lot to the final appearance of a casserole, soup,
or sauce. What we're talking about here is the total use of wine, from a
Ramos Chablis Fizz to Piccatas au Marsala.

WHAT? MIXED DRINKS WITH WINE?

Critics who recoil in horror from Spañada or Thunderbird un-
necessarily limit the range of tastes available to them. And their sense of

history is limited, too. The Greeks and Romans did all sorts of things to their wines, and in fact usually drank them with water. Next time you feel guilty about drinking white wine with ice cubes, think of Horace and his watered Falernian, forty years old, served on his fortieth birthday.

Champagne is, of course, a doctored wine. In the last century there was a craze in certain quarters, mainly Russia, for a *dosage* with enough sugar to make the residual amount 20 percent by volume! Fortunately, this mania passed. The great oenophile George Saintsbury, contemporary of H. Warner Allen, laid down the law: "Russe sweet champagne is fit only for savages or children." I've mentioned that vermouth and the German May wines are flavored with various spices—probably in the first instance to make a poor wine drinkable, but now with keen intent. So there's nothing wrong with a good sangria—that Spanish concoction of fruit and sweet red wine—and there's no reason why you can't make a punch like this of your own if you find yourself with a jug of red that doesn't quite do it for you.

How about *nonaccidental* use of wine in cocktails? Trader Vic calls them wine cups, and his basic recipe is adaptable to virtually any type of wine. He also mentions that the "medium sweetness of Ohio Valley wines" is his preference. But you can start with either a dry or a very sweet white, such as Muscato Amabile, or even a rosé. To a fifth (1.5 liters!) add an ounce of peach brandy, an ounce of Benedictine brandy, some mint, slices of an orange, and half a lemon. If you've started with a sweet wine, you can also add some strawberries and blackberries. This might be called a "white Sangria," and if, like me, you don't ordinarily happen to have peach brandy and Benedictine lying around the house, you can get by without it! That's the kind of recipe I like. Brandy is, after all, only a white wine with most of the water distilled out. But also remember that Trader Vic made his reputation on, among other things, the *precise* formulas for his exotic drinks. Too much variation from any recipe and you're just guessing.

The two most popular forms of wine cocktails are the simple spritzer and mulled wine. The former is simply a dry white wine and soda; the latter is red wine with cloves, lemon, and sugar, heated but not boiled. A cinammon stick for stirring and added flavor is a nice garnish. There are dozens of good recipes branching out from either of these white and red types. Trader Vic would have you add orange slices and flame it, and now it merits the fancier name "Vin Chaud." In the spritzer you can substitute a lemon-lime soda, or build it up to something more partyish by adding maraschino cherries or other fruit.

Here are some combinations that instinct alone could never lead you to: port and cranberry juice; pineapple juice, chilled tea, and muscatel; lemonade and Burgundy; eggnog and sherry. You can easily substitute a white wine in a "Gin" Fizz; a survey of Ramos Gin Fizzes in the San Francisco Bay Area turned up the startling fact that one of the more popular Sunday-brunch places mixes its fizzes with less than one percent alcohol. In all these drinks, what you taste is generally the fruit or the eggs and cream.

It seems to me that a jug wine you are happy with should be allowed to stand on its own two feet. Use it as a marinade, serve it as an aperitif, and offer it with the dinner. Mr. Allen's commentary on cocktails of all kinds puts the matter bluntly: "the cocktail—the crude mixed drink which is the enemy of wine and gods and men." Perhaps if the cocktail is made with a wine base it will not merit this rebuff.

THE ENVIRONMENT OF A WINE

Environment is quite a bit more than the glass or the carafe. Any wine tastes different with food than it does in a wine tasting, and most taste different with different foods. Who can judge this: doesn't wine also taste different when you're in a different mood? Mr. Allen approves of the admixture of a strong spice to wine, as a cocktail, if one is depressed or sorrowful, using as his authority the fact that Helen of Troy served such a potion to Telemachus "before the meal" when he and his comrades were grieving the loss of a friend. But then, what do you make of advice from a man who quotes Latin and Greek sources freely in his books without benefit of translation to English?

The very idea of having wine without food is a recent one. Pliny the Elder dismisses the cocktail as "a new and very undesirable fashion for persons engaged in important business and those who have to keep their wits about them. . . . Forty years ago, when Tiberius Claudius was Emperor, the custom of drinking on an empty stomach and taking wine regularly before meals came in, an outlandish fashion recommended by doctors who are always trying to advertise themselves by some newfangled idea." Down to our own day, the European custom has been to reserve other potions for aperitifs, or at least other types of wine: sherry, port, vermouth. But the Romans of Pliny's era didn't know about distillation and so had no sherry or port to sample.

When one knows what wine goes best with what foods—in cooking, not in dining—one is immediately liberated from a dependence on cookbooks. Each wine might be thought of as having its own best environment: Marsala with veal, Burgundy with beef, sweet Sauternes with salmon, rosé with prosciutto, claret with poached eggs, and Monsieur Raymond Oliver, owner of the three-star Grand Véfour in Paris, suggests Sancerre with pigeons. Well! With jug wines one can at least match the characteristics of the great vintages with the sugar or acid or body of the California version and make a reasoned guess. This is not a cookbook, but a few examples of the classic dishes in which wine is critical and not just pleasant will make the point clear.

Boeuf en daube, a casserole or what we normally think of as beef stew, has many variations, but the one proposed by Craig Claiborne best suits Virginia Woolf's implication in *To the Lighthouse:* "Everything depended upon things being served up the precise moment they were ready. The beef, the bay leaf, and the wine—all must be done to a turn. To keep it waiting was out of the question. Yet tonight, of all nights, out they went, and they came in late, and things had to be sent out, things had to be kept hot; the Boeuf en Daube would be entirely spoilt." Claiborne calls for the casserole to be arranged in layers of beef, vegetables, tomatoes, and mushrooms—piled one on top of the other until all the ingredients are used. The beef has been marinated in Burgundy and bay leaves (and also onion, garlic, thyme, salt, pepper, oil, and cognac—the usual), as have been the carrots and celery. The casserole is cooked in a cushion of bacon in the marinade. The beef can be browned after marinating or simply dredged in flour. Simple: but it's the wine working its wonder on the beef for two hours that makes the dish something more than beef stew. Boeuf Bourguignon is similar, but with potatoes instead of celery and a more complex preparation.

In France, a soup is traditionally prepared at harvest time for the grape pickers which has its roots in meat and fish stews, like bouillabaisse. Naturally, it features wine, and since the wine is a new one, even some recently fermented from the early picking, a big, raw jug of California "dago red" would be a reasonable equivalent. This one dish provides three courses: a soup, a drink, and a main course. Brisket of beef, veal bones, and a stuffed chicken are cooked slowly in a large pot, along with various vegetables and seasonings. The broth is strained off and served in bowls lined with stale bread; a mixture of the broth and the young wine is then drunk from the bowl; then the meats and vegetables are served.

Toulouse-Lautrec's cookbook brims with wine-flavored dishes, all the more delightful because the recipes proceed with Gallic disdain for scientific measurements and precise lists of seasonings. His "Leeks in Red Wine" is a model of a modest dish done with elán. Even though cold Vichyssoise is a marvelous soup that can be thinned again and again with an iced Chablis, the leek isn't a popular American vegetable. More's the pity. Lautrec's recipe calls for "a dozen or two leeks" cooked slowly in a casserole with red wine and a pound and a half of bacon, then browned in the oven with a covering of bread crumbs and sausage bits. The wine sauce is reduced to the point where "the leeks don't swim about," and the result is a creamy, mellow stew.

What does wine add to food in cooking? The alcohol quickly evaporates, leaving the minerals, liquid, and flavor of the wine in concentrated form. Even though cookbooks have been advising us for centuries to serve the same wine at dinner that has been used in cooking, we invariably "cheat"—assuming that a lesser wine will never be noticed in the dish. With a jug wine, of course, there's no reason to cheat. But there is a logic to keeping a consistent flavor throughout a meal, and if the original wine did have a distinct flavor it will be noticed.

In everyday wines, the sherries and ports leave the strongest suggestion of having been used in the cooking. No one will ever mistake the sherry in mushrooms sautéd lightly in butter and Livingston Cream. If you have ever had any doubts about the value of a wine in cooking, this dish will quickly remove them. And fortunately there are many good values in dessert wines; they're worth trying especially whenever a recipe calls for sugar and some other liquid! Here's a dessert, "German Wine Pie," which calls for any white wine and a third of a cup of sugar; obviously, you can cut down on the sugar or cut it out if you use a very sweet white wine:

> Separate four eggs, stirring a cup of sweet white wine into the beaten yolks. Add a teaspoon of gelatin and thicken by heating over a double boiler. Next beat the egg whites with a little salt and sugar as desired, and fold in the wine mixture and a half cup of whipped cream with vanilla flavoring. Pour into a pastry shell and chill. That's it!

PHOBIAS AND FOIBLES

Many a hostess takes her dinner menu to the local wine merchant for advice on the "right" wine for each course. Pulling at his beard, he leads her up and down the aisles touting the merits of this and that vintage. In the end she settles for something that's a "good price" and takes it home in fear and trembling—especially if rumor has it that one of her guests knows something about wine.

One way to beat "right-wine phobia" is to stick with jugs. You can then have plenty on hand, both red and white, so that you can offer an alternative to anyone who shows a preference. In reality, few wine buffs care that much about a particular wine with a particular food, and even the most sophisticated can't distinguish between the varietals. The black-glass test I mentioned earlier would show that many people can't tell the difference between a red and a white!

The Journal of Enology and Viticulture recently published a study at the University of California at Davis that showed how the experts can easily be fooled. Nine tasters with an average of 19 years experience each in enology were given a Cabernet, a Zinfandel, a Gamay, and a Barbera to taste over a period of time. In a total of 93 samples, about one-fourth of the time the tasters thought the Cabernet was a Zinfandel, and only a third of the time correctly identified it. The Zinfandel was recognized just half the time, and the Gamay only one out of twenty times! The Barbera was called a Cabernet twice as often as it was correctly picked.

Another three-star restaurant owner, Paul Bocuse, recently toured the United States to promote French cuisine and the simpler style of cooking he is pioneering. His practice is to take a walk in the morning to the local meat market and fish emporium and *there* decide what he will serve for lunch. At a stop in Los Angeles, he shocked his prominent guests by producing a red snapper cooked in a California red wine—and accompanied by the same wine! It was, he explained, the best buy at the market, and he simply decided to see how it would go with a big red wine. Which wine with which course? Simple, he said: stay with one for the entire meal. "You can have a very good meal with just a single course—just as you can have a very good meal with a single wine." How about salad? Don't the French always serve it last to avoid a conflict between the wine and the vinegar in the dressing? "People always say you shouldn't drink wine with salad, but why? Because there is vinegar in the salad? But if that were true, you shouldn't drink wine when you have a sauce béarnaise either."

But the taste buds are delicate, and lemon juice or a lot of vinegar can put them to sleep like a martini. One solution, other than to go light on the dressing, is to substitute Italian sweet vermouth for the lemon juice or the vinegar. Or use Pietro Pinoni's recipe, which is really a good mustard and garlic mayonnaise with a red wine instead of the vinegar. About the only food that has been discovered to go poorly with wine is a mushroom known as coprinus attramentarius; I am told that one can become quite ill—whether from the mushrooms or the wine—by feasting on one of these with a glass of wine.

There is another bugaboo I have already referred to as dry-wine elitism; it might also be called King Tut's Legacy. A large number of wine bottles were found in the pharaoh's tomb, and when the markings on them were decoded it was discovered that only four bottles were marked "sweet." What is one to do if one likes sweet wine? Drink it, of course, but check your taste buds from time to time to make sure you're not getting a hankering for drier versions. Above all, don't complain about a dry wine being vinegary; it probably isn't—but very dry wines do appear to have gone "off" to someone who habitually drinks sweet wines. And don't think you have to confine your sweet-wine drinking to the dessert course. It may not be to your taste, but for many Frenchmen a cream sherry or even a rich port is an excellent aperitif. Likewise, with a fiery hot curry a good choice for an accompanying wine is a Madeira, and possibly a drier sherry with a milder curry.

Temperature is an even simpler matter—there are few rules. Yet people continue to worry about whether a red wine is at room temperature or not, and they actually buy thermometers to be sure! This is like doing a chemical analysis of your food to see if it's salty or not. Foibles of temperature were more widespread in the last century than now; it was thought that a red wine should be quite warm (in English circles), and there was a silly practice of cooling and warming wines in the belief that this brought out the flavor. George Saintsbury laid this one to rest with characteristic flourish: "Icing good claret at all, is, as has been said, barbarous; but the idea of subjecting it to a process of alternate freezing, thawing, and freezing again is simply Bolshevist." If you like warm beer, you might also prefer warm white wines; but the simple rule is that the freshness and cleanness of a white wine are enhanced by a good chill, and let everything else take care of itself.

Finally, there is much folklore about the relative merits of white and red wine *for your health*. Some years ago, the French actually tried to test the varying theories about the benefits of red wine. A substantial number of subjects were divided into six groups, three drinking red and three white. A third of the subjects drinking red had two liters a day (!), another third one liter, and the rest just a glass or two; similarly for the white wines. At the end of six months it was found that the healthiest of the six groups was the middle range of the reds—the ones who drank a liter a day. The most unhealthy were the two-a-day drinkers of the whites. Yet even the subjects who drank a liter of white a day were better off than those who drank only a glass of either wine. It should be pointed out that there was very little control over previous eating and drinking habits.

Nevertheless, there is a good deal of data on the general beneficial effects of wine drinking—in moderation. Like any other form of drinking, the intake of wine is an intake of calories in the alcohol; when someone receives as much as 40 percent of his caloric intake from alcohol, he is an alcoholic by definition. It's malnutrition rather than brain damage that kills a "wino." A Moscow scientist recently published the results of a long-term study of 20,000 older residents of Georgia in the USSR. More than 2,000 of them were past their hundredth birthday! Five common elements appeared as indicators of longevity: no smoking, a large family, hard work, spicy foods, and a little wine daily. Perhaps the spicy foods required the wine, or vice versa—but there you have it. And something similar is going on in the Medoc district of France—the large claret-producing center. Wine is more a part of the daily diet here than in the rest of the country, yet there are twice as many octogenarians here per 100,000 population. A

French physician, who is seventy-four years old, has taken Gallic scholar-
ship to new heights by prescribing, in his *Wine is the Best Medicine*,
specific vintages for particular ailments.

One medical fact we know for certain: wine is a good tranquilizer.
Perhaps we didn't need to know why, other than the fact that it depresses
the central nervous system. But now along comes a pharmacologist at the
University of Missouri who has identified a compound called ellegic acid,
which is found in wine, beer, and the hulls of many nuts—but not in
unfermented alcoholic beverages. Ellegic acid is such a strong tranquilizer
that fishermen in the Ozarks cause fish to stumble to the surface by tossing
walnut hulls into the river.

Wine does contain many trace elements, such as iron. Because it's a
natural flavoring, it can reduce your dependence on salt. In many recipes,
a sweet wine can also reduce your need for sugar; you can make a spongy
pound cake by substituting a cup of Cream Sherry and instant pudding
mix for the sugar. Your jugs of wine belong in the kitchen—next to the
aspirin, the olive oil, and the stemware that resembles Helen's divine
breasts.

8

Improving the Breed

Pour your brandy through the air into a bathtub or other large receptacle, from the top of the stairs, for example. Then put the vile stuff into bottles, with a plum in each, and let it stand without a cork for a week or three. Now add a single drop of maraschino liqueur to each bottle and seal it. You'll have fine old brandy. Now you can give it a funny name and drink it out of big round glasses, rolling it around, warming it with your hands, and smelling at it like a dog.

—Hilaire Belloc

Wine is not as delicate a thing as we have talked ourselves into believing. After all, its first purpose in the days before refrigeration was to preserve grape juice from spoiling. Oxidation, aided by heat above 70° F. or so, is the only thing that can make a wine go bad; so in ancient days a proper stopper and shelter from the sun were sufficient to keep wine around for years. Somehow, in the Dark Ages, the harvesting and use of corks were lost as arts, and we find little in the literature between Roman times and the late Middle Ages about the glories of wine. Henry VIII drank his claret from bottles that had been stuffed with rags for closure, and the "cork finish" did not reappear until the time of Dom Perignon, the monk who concocted champagne.

This chapter is about concoctions. The purists of Dom Perignon's day no doubt railed against the new effervescent wine being put under the cork by this experimenter. But it took a cork to control the pressure of the *frisson.* And it took champagne to bail out the French wine industry in the 1880s when the phylloxera attacked the Bordeaux and Burgundy root stock. Pinot Noir was pressed into service to make a dry white wine subject to a second fermentation in the bottle, and thus was born Taitinger Blanc de Blanc, Dom Perignon, and several other sparkling wines that have put the Champagne region on the map.

Are there such things as jug champagnes? By our definition, yes; I've mentioned Setrakian as an excellent middle-of-the-road choice; there are also magnums from most major bottlers. And especially in California you'll see champagnes from the major makers, such as Weibel, put out under the label of the local liquor store, in magnums at a reasonable price (five to six dollars for 1.5 liters). But there are also things you can do to ordinary jug wines to *simulate* champagne—and a lot of other things.

THE CALIFORNIA 75

In World War I the French 75 was the finest gun at the front, and it soon became synonymous with the finest cocktail at the rear. A sugar cube drenched in cognac and champagne—there was a drink! Here's a recipe for making a jug of French 75, or, if you hold the brandy a little, a very good imitation of champagne:

Magnum of good white wine (1.5 liters)
Pint of brandy
Two quarts of sparkling water
   Mix ingredients and chill, or, better, freeze the wine and sparkling water before mixing. Yield: one full gallon of champagne. No ice, please. Pour from punch bowl into fifths with help of funnel for more elegant serving and to preserve bubbles.

The "California 75" depends on the quality of the ingredients. The white wine especially should be dry if you want a dry champagne; there's no way to disguise sweetness in this drink. If you've ever tasted a good Champagne gone flat, you've tasted a good dry white wine. As I've mentioned, the dryness is so important in a champagne that special grapes, such as the Burger, not of much use elsewhere, are excellent here. The French pick their grapes destined for champagne at less than 20 percent Brix, or sugar content, whereas most wines are made from grapes picked only after they reach 22 percent, ideally 24. Also choose a sparkling water you expect to bubble as long as possible. The brandy can be any acceptable label of your choice.

No need to apologize for your concoction; it's better than most of the cheap champagnes and a real cocktail, to boot. Now, if you want the pop of a cork, you'll have to improvise with a bottle corker and some masking tape—which brings us to:

ELEGANT SERVICE OF JUG WINES

What do you do when a party of six or eight expects to be served wine at your dinner? You go out and buy three or four expensive bottles of French or California wine, right? You can't plop a squat jug on the table very gracefully. Magnums are one solution, but even here you're paying quite a bit for the shape of the bottle, and usually the cork that goes along with it. It's not fair to fool your guests by rebottling jug wine in fancy fifths—though this is done in the best circles. What to do?

Save good fifths, such as the French type with concave bottoms. Carefully remove all labels and wash. For any given dinner or luncheon, put aside enough bottles of the same kind for your guests. One big exception: add a few more bottles for cocktails. When serving cocktails, let everyone know what's in the bottles. Then pour your favorite jug wine into the fifths with the help of a funnel and put them on the table with a cork lightly tapped in place. For your own use, you may want to bottle some of the jug wine in fifths by knocking corks fully into place with a four-dollar hand corker. (If there isn't a wine supply store near you, you can try any good-sized Italian hardware store in a metropolitan area.) There's no need to wrap the bottles in a towel or otherwise try to disguise the anonymity of the bottles. The idea of serving the same wine from cocktails through dinner is time-honored, and allows you the opportunity to explain to your guests that this is your choice and not a subterfuge.

The solution preferred by our wealthier neighbors is to have two or three good carafes on hand and simply deposit them on the table, filled, without the merest reference to what the wine may be. There's nothing wrong with this device as long as the jug wine is a good one. Which technique you prefer depends on your own tastes and the expectations of your guests. But the time is past when a host had to disguise his chosen wine for fear it would not measure up in prestige or price to the pedigree of his guests.

Since white wines are the drink of choice for aperitifs and often for any kind of dinner, a third solution is suggested. Ice a half gallon (or 1.5 liter jug) in an appropriate bowl and serve your white wine directly from the jug. The ersatz wine bucket can create enough of an effect on its own to overcome any latent wine snobbery in your party. This is especially true if the jug represents some effort on your part: it may be a varietal you had to search all over town for; it may be something available only at the winery; it may be a new wine your guests have never seen, picked up on a trip or requested especially from your local wine merchant. In any case, the care you have put into the selection will more than make up for its lack of "breeding."

FOR THE AROMA THAT "FILLS THE ROOM"

There are some things you *won't* want to try on your guests until you have perfected them, and even then you'll want to announce it well in advance. I'm talking about artificial aging and scenting. That's right, there are ways to give a jug wine a bigger bouquet and an oak "nose." If you've ever had the opportunity to sample one of the magnificent Château wines of the twenties or thirties, you know it's the experience of a lifetime—and there are ways to recapture a little of it.

Once I attended one of the annual wine auctions sponsored by the owners of Beaulieu and Inglenook, whose wines of the fifties and early sixties resembled the big clarets of France, and discovered I had arrived a little late for the "tasting" of the great vintages that were to be auctioned off. At some of these affairs, one bottle from a group of cases was ceremoniously opened and doled out to a cluster of eager samplers, who held their empty glasses aloft like beggars with uplifted tin cups. When a pre-1900 Château Lafite was opened, there was bedlam. And rightly so; hours later, the empty bottle still exuded a perfume that literally filled the room. Here I was late, however, with the auctioning about to begin. But this time there had been a different method of "tasting," and on a long, immaculate table in the center of the room were thirty or forty large snifting glasses each filled a quarter full with sea-dark wine. I wandered around the table examining the labels on the bottles. A 1929 Cheval Blanc stood modestly between an Haut Brion and a later Lafite. No one was tasting—I couldn't believe it. So I calmly raised a glass of "the noblest vintage of the twentieth century" to my lips. And around the table I proceeded, not draining the glasses by any means, but taking a good sip of each. After I had made nearly a complete circuit of the table, downing in the space of a few minutes perhaps fifteen hundred years of aging as if it were Mountain Castle, a guard approached me. In a very British tone, he advised, "I'm sorry, sir, but the wines are for snifting only, not for drinking." I winked at him and apologized, but the damage—or the ecstasy—was done.

Aerating wine, as Mr. Belloc suggests, does age it. The problem with such rapid aging is that you can go beyond the point of no return—oxidation—very quickly. At a recent International Conference of Peaceful Uses of Atomic Energy, fifteen Soviet scientists announced they had been able to age brandy in ten days by irradiation. This is indeed making wine, not war. There may be a bit of overkill here, however, since the average jug wine drinker doesn't have sources of radiation lying around the house. But they also reported another method: the use of oak shavings in the brandy. Now we have something.

If wine draws tannins and other flavorants from the walls of oak barrels, why not from oak chips? It does, and there are now sources for French or Yugoslavian oak chips in this country (see Appendix). Oak, in itself, doesn't signify age. Age, after all, means nothing if the wine is either chemically inert or has no tannin in it to begin with. All wines are heavily filtered these days, and, just as a tight titration of coffee removes a lot of the flavor with the sludge, heavy filtering reduces the tannins and other trace elements that give wine "aging potential." Why so much filtering? To make the wine less astringent, more drinkable right now for our "right now" generation of wine drinkers. Jug wines are bound to be low in "aging potential." With oak chips you can give back to the wine the tannins that the vintner took out!

But that aroma that fills the room and calls for words like supple and silken can't be bought in the drugstore.

DOCTORING

Over the years all sorts of things have been tried to induce that unmistakable aroma of age. The Romans used to "smoke" their red wines and seal the six-gallon amphorae with as much smoke as possible captured at the top. Alternate heating and chilling has been tried, to the consternation of people like H. Warner Allen; perhaps the theory was that if long winters and hot summers age people, it might work as well with wine. Realistically speaking, it's better to put fruit in it.

The price of raisins being what it is, one doesn't know whether he's basting the raisins or sugaring the wine—but adding raisins to red wines or port has been known to help both foods. I think it's a dead-end process; it's better to make your own wine than to try to remake it. (Again, I suggest the use of grape concentrate if you can't find good grapes in your vicinity. That failing, you can attempt a wine from any sort of fruit, as long as you get the sugar up to the point where fermentation can begin. H. L. Mencken wrote to his friend Harry Rickel, "I shall make some dandelion wine if I can find a dandelion. But down here they are not to be trusted. Dogs always piss on them. Also, now and then, a policeman.") No one really knows if a jug wine will age or not, because no one has ever tried it. There's something Charles Adamsish about a wine cellar stocked with half gallons, but why not? Aging is faster in smaller containers (more surface for the volume), so you might transfer the jug wine to fifths. Are corks necessary for aging? This is debatable, and that fact in itself is good news. The enologists at Gallo assure me that a cork closure is about as airtight as a screw cap: the only difference is the interaction between the small amount of air in the cork itself (and the trace elements in the cork) with the wine. The theory used to be that minute amounts of air are allowed to enter through the porous fibers of the cork, just as air enters through the oak staves into wine in barrels. It's good that there's still a lot we don't know about the creation of wine and its growth to maturity.

Wine can be doctored in other ways, too, that are less patient than cellar aging, but better than smoking it. If you chance by a vineyard, help yourself to a bunch or two and squeeze the berries into a jug wine. The yeast on a few grapes is sufficient to start a fermentation, but you won't get anything bubbling away unless you have a small barrel full. Yet the addition of good, fresh grapes to a jug wine can add quite a bit of flavor—crushed or not. Many people soak grapes in wine vinegar and report there's a smoothness that makes all the difference in salad dressings as a result. Vinegar is, after all, one of the wine types, and not a mistake. When wine goes sour, it's simply "vappa," as the Romans used to say—nothing.

Wine has a way of doctoring itself. It won't go bad if the alcoholic content is high enough to kill the errant yeasts. This is why you can leave a bottle of sherry or port open indefinitely, without fear of oxidation. But it will continue to evaporate if left open, and so the concentration of flavors will increase.

There's a curious race going on here. In a table wine, the alcoholic content is about 12 percent. If a third of the wine evaporates through the cork (this is called ullage), the percentage goes up to 18. This is sufficient to fortify the wine against attacks by the yeast that would turn the wine sour. But as the liquid evaporates, air necessarily enters the bottle, thereby throwing more oxidizing agents in contact with the wine. Who gets there first, the alcohol or the oxygen?

A few years ago I attended the wedding of a young couple whose parents included a couple celebrating their twenty-fifth wedding anniversary. The highlight of the affair—in my mind, at any rate—was a bottle of champagne that the parents had saved from *their* wedding. What would a 1948 bottle of Gallo Pink Champagne be like after twenty-five years? We popped the cork, but there was no pop. We poured the darkish liquid into glasses: not a bubble remained. Then we tasted it—it was like a fine old sherry. The alcohol had won the race!

At about the same time I received an emergency call from a friend who was restoring an old house. In the basement he had discovered two old wine barrels and thought he should consult an "expert" before he went near them. Feeling something like a member of a bomb squad, I crawled across the dirt floor toward the two barrels. My flashlight caught the bung hole—it was wide open. Well, so much for fine old wine, I thought. Then I rotated the barrel on its side and let a little liquid spill out into my hand. It was a heavenly port, as rich as prunes and as silken as a rare cognac. The barrels held only a few quarts of liquid, but it was a rare treasure indeed. In the end, the bottom of the barrel contained a sludge that would barely drop through the bung hole. I scooped it up like melted chocolate in my hands and funneled it into a wide-mouthed jar—the very essence of the wine. The magic liquid is now resting at the bottom of a small barrel in my basement, "teaching" some young ports the wisdom of age.

Many jug wines are simply sheep in sheep's clothing. They can't be taught by an older wine, they can't be doctored, they can't age on their own. The whites, in particular, are things to be drunk, and quickly. It may be true that California whites in jugs are, dollar for dollar, more impressive than California reds. This is the considered opinion of both amateur and professional tasters. But the reason for this is that jug reds are somehow stunted by the very fact of being thrust out into the world before their appointed time. Reds are supposed to be aged. And this fact points to the one trend that is yet to come, but it must: the vintage-dating of jug reds. It's a matter of storage space. When wineries have enough storage tanks or simply warehouses to store barrels, reds will not be put into bottles until they're three years old. What do we have today? Premium varietals released to market with a vintage date that shows them to be less than three years old.

When all other means of improving the breed of your jug wine are impractical, one avenue remains. Romance. For several years I have adopted the practice of printing or writing a special kind of label to be affixed to the back of special bottles of wine. It may be a birthday wine, or a bottle I'm bringing to a friend's house by surprise, or the token bottle one is supposed to bring to a dinner party. In any case there's always something one wants to say to the hosts, and a label on a bottle of wine is a unique way of saying it—especially if the bottle is going to be on the table at dinner. Then, as it's passed around and poured, the statement you have made becomes a topic of conversation. In other cases, it can be as light as a birthday card. On a bottle of Sancerre, it might be the opening lines of *The Old Man and the Sea*. On a jug wine, it might be a Woody Allen joke. For me, wine in itself calls for something ringing, stirring, singing, like Emile Zola's epitaph to Dreyfus:

> What matter the errors of fate or the false directions in life if a few fervent and luminous hours give meaning to a lifetime?

Appendix

I: INDEX OF DOMESTIC AND IMPORTED JUG WINES, WITH CAPSULE EVALUATIONS

This section can be used as a quick reference and as an index to the text. The evaluations are primarily the author's, supplemented by comments from newsletters and various tastings. Most of the California wineries produce three standard types: Burgundy, Chablis, and rosé. Unless otherwise noted, or unless one of these is singled out for comment, these types are assumed to be available from each large California winery and are not listed. Many of these wines are available in fifths (750 milliliter) as well as 1.5 liters, 3 liters, and so forth; some are only in fifths and may even be cork-finished, but are listed as jug wines because of their "everyday" character (see the guidelines for jug wines in chapter 1). I have included New York State wines, even though most of them cannot be considered jug wines, and I have arbitrarily omitted the products of other states because they are not yet generally available. Many of the New York wines, however, are generally available and may soon be sold in jugs; the state now produces more than ten percent of that of California's booming wineries, and an increasing quantity of California grapes can be expected to be used in Eastern production. Distribution of imports varies greatly throughout the country, so I have listed only a sampling of the major brands appearing on both coasts.

The absence of an evaluation implies only that there is no clear-cut comment worth making, and does not reflect on the quality of the wine.

Symbols are used as follows as a shorthand for common remarks; where necessary I have spelled out other comments:

CHARACTERISTICS

A touch of sweetness, semi-sweet, etc., in table wines

Unusually dry, low residual sugar, etc.

Full-bodied, heavy, well-rounded, etc.

= ▱

= □

= ○

Thin, exceptionally light, lacking in taste, etc.   = |

Astringent, tart, acidic, sharp, etc.   = △

Smooth, no aftertaste, quite mellow, etc.   = —

Noticeable aroma or bouquet   = ∼

(Note: no symbol can do justice to such broad descriptions; this is only a guide to your own tasting.)

COMMENTS

Exceptional value, a "discovery," excellent for the money   = ✓

Budget wine, without great merit except for price   = ¢

On the expensive side, may not be worth the difference to you   = $

Pronounced varietal character, ample fruit   = ⚭

Honored in competitions or tastings, well recommended   = ⌂

Popular favorite over many years, and deservedly so   = ★

May be difficult to find, available only at winery, etc.   = ⊏⊐

Vintage-dated, shows signs of good aging, etc.   = ◖

A fortified wine, 18–20 percent alcohol   = %

MAJOR IMPORTS, BY REGION,
TYPE, OR MAKER

	Characteristics	Comments
Alexis Lichine Table White	○ □	⌂ $
Amedeo Fancelli (white)	|	
Anselmi Valpolicella (red)	○	⚭ $
Banfi (see Villa Banfi)		
Bardolino (see Fresco Baldi or Della Scaldi)	| □	
Barolo (see Bersano—there are many good makers)		
Bersano (several reds)	○ ⬠	$
Biscardo Soave (white)	△ □	
Bolla Soave	△ □	★
Bon Frere Blanc	△	

Il Frascati
di Monteporzio Catone
SECCO

Frascati
Superiore
Denominazione di origine controllata
imbottigliato dalla
Cantina Soc. di Monteporzio Catone Coop. r. l.
MONTEPORZIO CATONE
ITALIA
0,720 LITRI   12°/₄ VOL
RI869 ROMA

NET CONTENTS   ALCOHOL 11.5%
1.5 LITER   BY VOLUME

PRODUCT      OF ITALY

SOAVE

DENOMINAZIONE D'ORIGINE CONTROLLATA

 ®

BOTTLED BY S.V.I. S.p.A. - PERSICO DOSIMO - ITALIA - FOR
F.LLI FOLONARI ANTICA CASA VINICOLA S.p.A. - BRESCIA

Imported by
CARLTON SALES COMPANY · NEW YORK, N.Y.

PRINTED IN ITALY

FOLONARI
TRADE MARK   SINCE 1825
DRY WHITE WINE

	Characteristics	Comments
Burgella, Juan Hernandez (red)	○	¢
Calli Albani (red)	△	
Cantina Valpiave (white)				
Capezzani (red) 1.75-liter size		$
Casa Bruciato (white)	△	
Chalais, Juan Hernandez (white)		¢
Chantefleur (white)	△	$
Chianti, Montalbano (many makers)	□	⌄
Del Ventuno (red)	△	
Della Scala—Soave, Valpolicella, etc.		⌄
Ecu Royale Country White	○ ▱	✿ ⌂ ⌄
Faustino V (Spanish)	○ —	
Folonari Soave	—	☆ ⌄
Fontana Candida (white)			$
Fortuna Soave		
Frascati	□	⌂
Fresco Baldi, Valpolicella, Bardolino, etc.	○	
La Cove Victori, Petit Fleur	△	
La Fleur Blanche	□ △	
Lambrusco (many makers)	▱ ▱		☆
Opici Verdicchio (red)		
Princeps (white)	▱ ~	
Remy Pannier Blanc de France			$
Rioja (many makers in this region)		—	☆ ⌄
Roman Red (and White)			
San Vito Soave, Valpolicella, etc.		
Soave (see Bolla, etc.)		
Sole di Roma	△ ~	¢
Torres (reds)	○ —	$

	Characteristics	Comments
Valpolicella (many makers, see above)		
Valtellina		
Vignolle (white)	▢	**$**
Villa Banfi, Segesta (many other Italian types)	◯	★

NEW YORK STATE WINES, BY WINERY OR DIVISION

(See pages 100–102)

	Characteristics	Comments
Barry Wine Company (see O-Neh-Da)		
Boordy Vineyards (red, white, rosé, and sweet white)		Eastern-type hybrids
Brotherhood, Delaware, Catawba, etc.	▱	Eastern-type hybrids
Bully Hill (red, white, rosé, types)	▢	Eastern-type hybrids
Canadaigua Industries, Richard's Wild Irish Rose, Virginia Dare, etc.	◯	also some available fortified ⚮
Gold Seal, Catawba Pink and White	▱ —	Excellent champagnes
Great Western (see Pleasant Valley Wine Company)		
Hargrave	▢	Long Island vinifera wines **$**
High Tor (Rockland Red)	◯	currently inactive
Hudson Valley Wine Company		Eastern-type hybrids
Johnson Estate, Dry White, Red; Vin Rouge Kedem (see Royal Winery)	△	also Eastern-type hybrids
Manischewitz (Monarch Wine Co.) (kosher)	▱ ▱ —	now also into drier types ★
Marlboro Industries (kosher)		Eastern-type hybrids

	Characteristics	Comments
Mogen David (1.5- and 3-liter sizes) (kosher)	▱ ▱ —	also pop-type wines ★
O-Neh-Da	▱ ▱ —	sacramental wines only
Pleasant Valley Wine Company (various, broad list)		exceptional house wine available only on-sale, excellent champagnes ✔
Royal Winery	▱ ▱ —	another kosher winery
Schapiro	▱ ▱ —	a kosher winery in Manhattan
Taylor (a complete line of vinifera and Eastern-type hybrids)		Rhine, Sauterne, Burgundy labels as well as champagnes, sherries, and ports. All moderately sweet, but with aging quality in the reds.

Widmer's (also a complete offering, with sherries, ports, vinifera table wines, and the Eastern Niagara, Salem, Dutchess, etc.)

CALIFORNIA WINES, BY MAKER, REPRESENTATIVE SAMPLE

Almadén Vineyards, page 40 The winery lists its table wines in five categories: mountain, generics, standard varietals, classic varietals, and special selection vintage, in ascending order of price. The first three fall into the everyday wine category, in magnum, 3- and 4-liter sizes. The most widely available are:

	Characteristics	Comments
Zinfandel	—	
Chenin Blanc (Grenoir Original)	▢	
Grenache Rosé		☍

	Characteristics	Comments
Mountain Red Burgundy		
Mountain White Chablis		
Mountain Rhine		★
Mountain Nectar Vin Rosé		
Solera Cream Sherry		%
Solera Cocktail Sherry		★△%

Amador Winery, page 95

Madam Pink Chablis		
Mountain Jubilee		
Sutter's Gold		

Assumption Abbey Winery

| Dessert wines of many types from Angelica to Cream Marsala | | % |

Astor House, page 45

| The house brand of a large New York liquor store, made by the Bear Mountain Winery at Arvin, California | | |
| Red, white, and rosé types | | |

Barengo Vineyards, page 52

Vintner's Reserve, standard types		
Dudenhoefer Spiced and May Wines		
Vino Mio		
The Barengo Reserve varietals and table wines (Chablis, Burgundy, etc.) are priced about the same as the Vintner's Reserve and are easier to find.		
Crema Marsala		$ △%

	Characteristics	*Comments*
Bargetto, page 52		
Tawny Port, Cream Sherry	▱ ▱	$ ▭ ⌂ %
Various fruit wines	▱ ▱	🍎 ▭ ⌂
Beringer (Los Hermanos), page 33		
Malvasia Bianca	▱ ▱	$ ☆ ❦
Los Hermanos Mountain Burgundy	—	☆
Bertero, page 52		
Zinfandel	◯ —	$ ▭ ❦ %
Bronco Wine Company, page 37		
CC Vineyard, standard types	❘	¢
JFJ Winery, Rhinewine	▱ ❘	¢
Ruby Rosé, Cabernet, Rich Burgundy		▭ ✓
Sangria		🍎
Chablis	◯	✓
Brookside Vineyard Co.		
Various fruit-flavored wines, including an award-winning chocolate (!)	▱ ▱	🍎 ▭ ⌂ ✓
Vino Rosso	◯ —	
Sangria and Sangria Blanca	◯	🍎 ▭ ⌂
Buena Vista, page 74		
Chablis	▢ ❘	$
California Growers Winery, Inc., page 45–47		
Growers Burgundy, Sauterne, etc.	—	☆ ⌂ ✓
Setrakian Champagne	▢	▭ ⌂ ✓
Growers, various fortified wines	▱ ▱	⌂ %
Setrakian Mountain Vin Rosé	◯	▭

	Characteristics	*Comments*
Setrakian Brandy	—	△%
Bounty Brandy	—	⊑△%
Setrakian Solera Cream Sherry	▱▱	⊑△↙

California Wine Association, page 36

(Perelli-Minetti Winery)

A. R. Morrow Brandy	—	★△%
Guasti Champagne	☐	⊑△↙
Ambassador Champagne Guasti Rhine	▱	⊑△
Guasti, various fortified wines	▱▱	△%

Cambiaso Vineyards, page 35

| 1852 House Wine Burgundy | ☐◯ | ⊑ |

Ceremony Brandy Cellars

| Ceremony Brandy | | ★△% |

Charles Krug, page 22

See C. K. Mondavi; only the "C. K." label offers jug wines.

Christian Brothers, page 22

| Napa Rosé | ◯ — | $ |

(Also Burgundy and Chablis in 4-liter size, to on-sale accounts only)

Cresta Blanca, page 34

Mendocino Zinfandel	☐ —	⊑◔△
North Coast Burgundy		
Grenache Rosé	◯	◔

Cribari & Sons, page 36

| Famiglia Cribari Vino Bianco Da Pranza | ◯ | |

	Characteristics	Comments
Mendocino Burgundy	│ — ∼	⋀ $
Brandy		⋀
Cucamonga Vineyard Company		
Champagne		▭ ⋀
Petite Sirah	◯	▭ ⋀
d'Agostini, page 95		
Zinfandel	◯ —	▭ ⋀ ⚘
Davis Bynum,		
Red	—	▭
Delicato Vineyards, page 36		
Cabernet	◯	▭ ↙
Green Hungarian		▭ ⚘ ↙
Generics		¢
East-Side Winery, page 92		
Royal Host Brandy		⋀ %
Royal Host Dry Vermouth	▢	◔
Emilio Guglielmo, page 36		
Emile's Private Stock Blanc Sec	▢ ◯	★
Emile's Mellow Burgundy	▱ ◯	
Fetzer Vineyards, page 22		
Premium Red	▢ │ △	★ $
Premium White	▢	⋀ $
Mendocino Claret	▢ │	▭ $
Franciscan Vineyards, page 50		
North Coast Burgundy	◯	⋀ $
1977 California Chablis	▢	▭ ⋀ $

| | Characteristics | Comments |

Franzia Brothers Winemakers, page 44

  Franzia generics

  Franzia Wine Tap, 3- and 5-
    gallon containers for on-sale,
    above generics

  Yosemite Road varietals

E. & J. Gallo Winery, page 92–93

  Gallo generics

  Gallo Sauvignon Blanc

  Gallo Hearty Burgundy

  Gallo Chablis Blanc

  Carlo Rossi generics

  Spañada (sangria-type)

  Tyrolia (white)

Geyser Peak Winery, page 65

  Summit generics

  Also available in 3- and 5-gallon
    containers for on-sale.

Gibson Wine Company, page 65

  Old Fashion American Strawberry
    Wine

  Various dessert wines

In addition to the usual generics,
  this winery has some
  imaginatively labelled specialty
  wines: Candlelite Pink Chablis,
  Das Guten Rheinwein, Viva
  Italiano Vino

Giumarra Vineyards, page 36

  Mountain Burgundy, Chablis

This winery also offers some unusual
  hybrids developed for California's

	Characteristics	Comments
warmer growing regions, such as Carnelian and Ruby Cabernet	○ —	⋀ $
3- and 4-gallon pouches for on-sale use are available in the winery's generics.		

Guild Wineries, page 40

(See also Cresta Blanca and Cribari)

Guild offers three levels of jug wines: premium table, standard varietals, and classic varietals. An example of each

Cabernet Sauvignon	○ ▢	🄴 ⚲ $
Green Hungarian	▱	🄴
Mountain Nectar Vin Rosé	○ ▱	🄴
Vintner's Choice generics	▱ ❘	¢
Tavola Red, White, Rosé	○	☆

Hacienda Wine Cellars, page 89

| This is the new winery of the founder of Buena Vista, a stone's throw away. One of its wines might be considered an "everyday" one: Estancia Napa Valley Burgundy | ○ — | 🄴⋀ |

Harvest, page 64

| House wine of Lucky Stores, red, white, rosé | △ ❘ | ¢ |

Inglenook Vineyards, page 49

Navalle Burgundy	○ —	☆⋀
Navalle Cabernet Rosé	○ —	◔🄴⋀ $
Navalle French Colombard	▱	⚲

Italian Swiss Colony, page 31

| Colony Chablis | ○ — | ⋀ |
| Colony Chianti Red | ○ — | ⋀ |

Colony Cabernet Sauvignon

Rhineskeller Moselle

In addition to a wide variety of standard wine types, Colony also offers "refreshment wines" and generics under proprietary labels, such as Cappella, "the little chapel in the vineyard." The names are imaginative: T. J. Swann Mellow Days and Easy Nights, After Hours, Stepping Out, Bali Hai, and a sangria called Sangrole. Well known is:

	Characteristics	*Comments*
Annie Green Springs Cherry Country	▱ ▱	◌ ✓

Jacaré

This is the label of a proprietary blend from United Vintners, in distinctive, glazed bottles, in red, white, and rosé types — ▱

Kirigan Cellars, page 96

| Grenache Rosé | ◯ — | ▤ |

Llords & Elwood Winery, page 69

| Ancient Proverb Port | ◯ ▱ ▱ | ★ △ $ |

L. Le Blanc Vineyards, Inc.

| Le Blanc generics | ◯ ▢ | ¢ |
| Le Blanc Gold Chablis | ◯ ▢ | ¢ |

Lost Hills, page 70

| Lost Hills Cabernet Sauvignon | ◯ — | ▤ ✓ |

M. LaMont

| M. LaMont generics | ◯ | ⚭ |

Also many varietals at everyday prices

Martini & Prati Wines, Inc., page 89

| Martini & Prati generics | ▢ | |
| Martini & Prati Zinfandel | ❘ | ⚭ ✓ |

Monterey Peninsula Winery page 96

Though not a jug wine maker, any more than Llords and Elwood above, it's worth mentioning this winery to clarify some confusion. Mirassou uses "Monterey" on its labels to identify the source of some of its premium, award-winning wines. The Monterey Vineyard (south of Salinas) is a cooperative now owned by Coca-Cola and the producer of Taylor's California wines. The winery continues to produce under its own label as well. And "Monterey Cellars" on a label identifies the products of this smaller winery, such as:

	Characteristics	*Comments*
Emerald Riesling	○ ▱	⚘ ⌂ $
C. Mondavi & Sons, page 42		
CK Mondavi Barberone	○ —	⚘ ★
CK Mondavi Light Burgundy	｜ △	⌐
Fortissimo and Bravissimo	○ △	%
Mountain Castle		
House wine of Safeway Stores, red, white, rosé	△	¢
Novitiate Wines		
Chateau Novitiate (white)	▱ —	▭ $
Muscat Frontignan	▱ ▱	★ $ %
Oakville Vineyards		
French Colombard	○ —	▭ ⚘ $
Parducci Wine Cellars, page 34		
Vintage Burgundy	○ —	▭ ◗
Paul Masson Vineyards, page 59		
Rhine Castle Emerald Dry	▱ —	⚘ ★ $
Rosé	○	⚘
Sangria	○	▭ ◖
Pedrizzetti		
Barbera, N.V.	○ □	◗ ▭ ⚘ ⌐
Petri		
Petri generics	○	¢

	Characteristics	Comments
Marca Petri Pastoso	○ ⬭ △	
Rapazzini Winery, page 61		
Grenache Rosé	○ —	⚘ ⌂
Cream Marsala	▱ ▱	⬒ %
Red Mountain		
Gallo's bargain label		¢
Robert Mondavi Winery, page 89		
Red Table Wine	☐ △ |	★ $
White Table Wine	☐ △	⌂ ★ $
Carlo Rossi		
See Gallo		
Round Hill Cellars, page 89		
Chablis	○ ☐	⬒ ⌂ $
Royal Host		
See East-Side Winery.		
San Antonio Winery, page 97		
Special Mellow Burgundy	○ —	⬒ ⌂
May Wine	▱	⍟ ⬒ ⌂ ✓
San Benito· Vineyards, page 65		
Bing Cherry Wine	▱ ▱	⍟ ⌂
San Martin, page 96		
Vintage Burgundy	○	⬬ ⬒
Aprivette	▱ ▱	⍟ ⌂ %
Sebastiani Vineyards, page 62		
Sweet Rosé	○ ⬭	⬒ ⌂
Mountain Chablis	☐	⌂
Cabernet Sauvignon	○ ☐ —	⌂ $

Characteristics   Comments

Setrakian

  See California Growers.

Sonoma Vineyards, page 89

  Chenin Blanc

  Adequate White

Stony Ridge Winery, page 95

  Malvasia Bianca

Sutter Home, page 89

  California Burgundy

Trentadue, page 89

  1973 Sonoma Burgundy

Villa Armando Winery, page 91

  Rustico

Weibel Champagne Vineyards, page 91

  Green Hungarian

Note: This list is necessarily somewhat arbitrary in that I have included wines one would not ordinarily consider "jugs" because of their price, but which have points of interest worth mentioning or fill gaps in the repertoire of wine types (e.g., brandies). At the same time I have omitted many smaller wineries (e.g., Joseph Phelps) and some not so small (Beaulieu) for reasons of price. The following are some labels used by California wineries for out-of-state accounts, with the location of the winery or business office of the shippers: Aquino (Sonoma), Fior di California (San Francisco), Corona D-Oro (Manteca), Fortino (Gilroy), Gambarelli and Davitto (San Francisco), Opici (San Francisco), Orsini (Elk Grove), Roma (Lodi), Romano (Cucamonga). Generally speaking, these are budget wines of average or varying quality.

II: NEWSLETTERS, BOOKLETS, SLIDES, TAPES, TOURS, CLUBS, GROUPS, AND PRODUCTS RELATED TO WINE

NEWSLETTERS

Robert Finigan's Private Guide to Wines. Monthly $24 per year. Devoted mainly to fine wines, foreign and domestic, with occasional reviews of jug wines as a group. Thorough and knowledgeable, though definitely one man's opinion, as one would expect. Sample copy on request: 100 Bush Street, San Francisco, California 94104.

San Diego Grapevine. Bimonthly, $12 per year. Devoted to new releases of fine California wine. Detailed evaluations on the 20-point scale by a panel of wine merchants, writers, and buffs. One of the places to look for those rare "discoveries" before the gossip mill makes them scarce. Money-back guarantee: P. O. Box 22152, San Diego, California 92122.

Connoisseur's Guide to California Wines. Bimonthly, $20 per year. The most detailed and comprehensive "tip sheet" I've seen. Not intended for everyday wines, but the line is hard to draw much of the time as more good varietals go into magnums and 3 liter jugs. P. O. Box 11120, San Francisco, California 94101.

Wine Discoveries. "A Guide to Exceptional Wines Under Four Dollars," by Arthur Damond and Nick Scott. Bimonthly, $8.50 per year. A dozen or more "discoveries" are fully described and located in California stores—though not necessarily all California wines. But did you ever have the feeling that it's better that wines, like small restaurants, are best not "discovered" in print? Send self-addressed, stamped envelope for sample copy: 7474 Terrace Drive, El Cerrito, California 94530.

Bottles Up. "Fred Cherry's Personal Journal of Good Drinking." Monthly, $20 per year (with reduced rates for additional gift subscriptions, for groups, etc.). A two-page centerpiece of anonymous evaluations and Fred's ranking is only the beginning of this rambling, casual, and very unstuffy letter. There's something for everyone here, including a range of humor from the sly to the smirking. As the many comments throughout this book indicate, I find Cherry's approach to the enjoyment of wine the most sensible among the major critics in the country. Ninety percent of the letter is devoted to wine, in spite of the more general title. The Fred Cherry Company, 470 Columbus Avenue, San Francisco, California 94133.

California Wine Advisor. "An Inside View: Written and Privately Distributed By Perelli-Minetti Winery." Bimonthly, free on request. One of the better winery-sponsored newsletters in that it includes more than just puffery for its own products. Get on the mailing list at the winery, or write to them at Delano, California 93215.

Sebastiani Vineyards. Monthly, free on request. An honest, informational four-page newsletter on the wine-making process, recipes, new releases, and anything else that interests Sam Sebastiani, who, we understand, takes a personal hand in the writing. P. O. Box AA, Sonoma, California 95476.

Sterling Vineyards. Bimonthly, free on request. Tasting notes and occasional news about Sterling releases, and order forms (Sterling is one of the few wineries doing a good mail-order business). P. O. Box 365, Calistoga, California 94515.

The Wine Scene. Ten issues annually, $15. Sample issue, $2. Expert evaluations by critic John D. Movius, with emphasis on imported wines in contrast to the above. P. O. Box 49358, Los Angeles, California 90049.

BOOKETS, SLIDES, TAPES

Guide Beccaro. An illustrated guide to Italian wine types, featuring the Beccaro brands, of course. Send stamped, self-addressed envelope to Beccaro International, 1550 Rollins Road, Burlingame, California 94101.

Italian Wine Vintage Chart, Italian Wine Guide. The Italian wine industry is currently the most cooperative on the European scene, having recently upgraded their standards and wanting everyone to know about it. For these free guides write the Italian Wine Promotion Center, One World Trade Center, Suite 2057, New York, N.Y. 10048.

French Correspôndence Course. Free course on the wine producing regions of France. Write Foods From France, Inc., 1350 Avenue of the Americas, New York City, N.Y. 10019.

How to Test and Improve Your Wine Tasting Ability, by Irving S. Marcus. 96 pages, $2.95. An authoritative booklet by a well-known wine aficionado. Write Wine Publications, 96 Parnassus Road, Berkeley, California 94708.

Cocktails With Wine, by Penny Hightower. $3.95. A jolly, mouth-watering booklet with some 250 recipes. Write P. O. Box 8828, Anaheim, California 92802.

California Wine Atlas, 21 maps in full color. $9.95 (plus applicable state tax). Unbound, in folder; descriptive text and comprehensive listing of wineries, wine varieties, climates, grape acreage, etc. Write Ecumene Associates, P. O. Box 4313, Hayward, California 94540. (Inquire also about color slides of same material.)

French Wine Slides. A documentary on the regions of Alsace, Burgundy/ Rhone, and Bordeaux—220 slides, $99. Also available separately for the three regions. Write Patrice Gourdin, Les Amis du Vin, 85-35 58th Avenue, Elmhurst, New York 11373.

Wine Cassettes. Tapes on vocabulary, tastings, California, and France, $39.95. Also available separately at $9.95 each. Write Bunny Fredericks, Adventures in Wine, P. O. Box 06453, Portland, Oregon 97206.

Wine Pronunciation Cassette. Ninety-minute cassette (or reel-to-reel), covering European place names and wine terms, with 24-page index. $12.50 (and applicable state sales tax). Write Winetapes, P. O. Box 510, Corte Madera, California 94925.

CLUBS, GROUPS, AND TOURS

Les Amis du Vin. A nationwide club with some 200 chapters, offering tours, tastings, and a club newsletter. $15 per year. Write 2302 Perkins Place, Silver Springs, Maryland 20910.

Society of Wine Educators. Numerous chapters, especially active in California, offering classes, tastings, tours. Write 499 Hamilton Avenue, Palo Alto, California 94301 for further information.

The Wine Tutor. A wine-study vacation at The Wine Country Inn in the Napa Valley: four days of tasting, lectures, winery visits, etc. For brochure write 1423 Foothill Blvd. N., Calistoga, California 94515.

Wine Tours Overseas. Among the many vacations and cruises led by wine guides, prominent ones are offered by Bacchantes' Pilgrimages, 19687 Gary Avenue, Sunnyvale, California 94086; and The Travel Seller, 104 Petticoat Lane, Walnut Creek, California.

PRODUCTS

One would think that the only product necessary for the enjoyment of wine is a good corkscrew—and not even that with most jug wines. But there is a good deal of trivia that people will spend their money on if they have nothing better to do—and, who knows?—it may help them enjoy their hobby. In this category are such things are:

The Wine Belt. Sort of a simplified Swiss Army Knife around your waist—a leather belt with built-in-cork-puller, which will also remove bottle caps. If you can't remember to bring a corkscrew, at least you might remember to wear this belt. Write The Wine Belt Company, 10 Greenfield Drive, Moraga, California 94556.

The Bacchus Wine Opener. The search for the perfect corkscrew goes on! This is a solid brass, eight-pound contraption that clamps on a shelf and disgorges the cork with the pull of a handle. Write Bacchus-West, 211 Third Street, Pacific Grove, California 93950.

Le Bouchon. If you can't finish that bottle of champagne, stopper it with this gold-plated device. The Dobbe Company, P. O. Box 4990, North Hollywood, California 91607.

Wine Chiller. A refrigerant liner that allows you to chill wine without ice buckets, freezers, or overloading your refrigerator. Glacierware, Inc., P. O. Box 566, Bloomfield, Connecticut 06002.

Vinometer. Attention to temperature can be taken to extremes, but if you like precision, here's just the thing to tell you the centigrade in the bottle. Serendipity, University Village, 474 Howe Avenue, Sacramento, California 95825.

Wine Storage. There are as many ways to make racks for wine as there are rules for the perfect golf swing. Some of the simplest and best are described in a 12-page booklet available for 50¢ from Lousiana-Pacific Corp., 1300 S. W. Fifth Avenue, Portland, Oregon 97201. For self-contained security cabinets that also guarantee a uniform, low temperature, you might try either the Wine Vault (P. O. Box 6298, San Jose, California 95150), or the Time Machine (Vintage House, Inc., 1254 Montgomery Avenue, San Bruno, California 94066).

Wine Glasses. The simple, tulip-shaped glass with a relatively small opening at the top, holding about six to eight ounces, is the universal wine glass. It retains champagne bubbles longer and intensifies the bouquet of table wines. For something more elegant than those available on supermarket shelves, you might send for Marjorie Lumm's catalog ($1, refundable on purchase): P. O. Box 732, Sausalito, California 94965. The Mirassou Winery also offers fine, handmade sets. Inquire at 3000 Aborn Road, San Jose, California 95121.

Exotica. How about a T-shirt that proclaims "Life's too short to drink bad wine"? Available for $3.50 from Wollersheim Winery, Highway 188, Prairie du Sac, Wisconsin 53578. Or wallpaper featuring silk-screened reproductions of California wine labels? Inquire to Wine Line, 426 North Street #7, Healdsburg, California 95448.

Ironically, the jug wine drinker has more reason to experiment with products of a more serious nature than does the fine wine drinker. I refer to various "additives" that can be used to upgrade a bulk wine, as described in chapter 8. One can attempt to imitate the aged-in-oak flavor by adding wood chips or equivalent to a jug wine, or even balance the acidity/sugar by adding tartaric acid. Purists insist on French or Yugoslav oak chips, but it all depends on the original flavor of the wine. American oak goes well with many tannin-rich wines. So start by going to your woodpile, and experiment.

An improvement on chips is the granular form; it permeates the wine more evenly and quickly. You can buy chips or oak granules at any good wine supply store. One of the largest mail-order firms is Wine and the

People, 907 University Avenue, Berkeley, California 94710. You can also buy grape concentrate, fresh wine grapes, fermented wine in 5-gallon carboys (Zinfandel about $30, or a little more than $1 a fifth), and some very well finished premium wines here also. A pound of oak granules ($2.50) would easily handle five gallons, depending on your taste for oak! A 4-ounce package of "acid blend" would also be sufficient to "correct" five gallons of wine you feel is too sweet. Send for the Wine and the People catalog for the whole bag of tricks.

III: THE WINE GROWING REGIONS OF CALIFORNIA

As originally defined by the Enology and Viticulture departments of the University of California, five regions ranging from coolest to warmest have been established as guidelines to growers. Since prices of a particular grape variety tend to be higher in the cooler regions, the exact boundaries are important to growers and redefinitions occasionally are asked for. The advent of new hybrids developed specifically for warmer climates has lessened the importance of regions to consumers.

Region I: The North Coastal area, from San Francisco bay north in Napa, Sonoma, and Mendocino counties. Newer Region I locations near the coast have been established from the Monterey Peninsula south. The Pinot noir, White Riesling, and Chardonnay grapes are best grown in this region.

Region II: Cabernet and Merlot grapes thrive in this slightly warmer region, chiefly from Napa to Healdsburg, east of U. S. 101.

Region III: Further north, from Ukiah east, lies a typical example of this region, with climates similar to those around King City-Santa Barbara and parts of San Diego County at the bottom of the state.

Region IV: The northerly part of the Sacramento-San Joaquin Valley and areas around Cucamonga and Escondido in the south are still warmer. The University of California at Davis testing station is in this region.

Region V: The warmest and largest growing region of the state encompasses most of the valley south of Merced and north of Sacramento.

In all of the five regions there are pockets of climate that differ from the surrounding area. The Shenandoah Valley of Amador County is a good example; Zinfandels grown here rival—and some say exceed—the best in Region II.

IV: WINE LABELING REGULATIONS

From: Federal Register, August 23, 1978—excerpts that indicate further upgrading in quality of bulk wines.

4.23a Varietal (grape type) labeling (not Mandatory before January 1, 1983).

(a) *General.* The names of one or more grape varieties may be used as the type designation of a grape wine only if the wine is also labeled with an appellation of origin, as defined in 4.25a.

(b) *One variety.* The name of a single grape variety may be used as the type designation if not less than 75 percent of the wine is derived from grapes of that variety, the entire 75 percent of which was grown in the labeled appellation of origin area.

(c) *Exceptions.* (1) Wine made from any Vitis Labrusca variety (exclusive of hybrids with Labrusca parentage) may be labeled with the varietal name if: (i) Not less than 51 percent of the wine is derived from grapes of that variety; (ii) the statement "contains not less than 51 percent (name of variety)" is shown on the brand label, back label or a separate strip label. . . .

(d) *Two or three varieties.* The names of two or three grape varieties may be used as the type designation if: (1) All of the grapes used to make the wine are of the labeled varieties; (2) the percentage of the wine derived from each variety is shown on the label (with a tolerance of plus or minus 2 percent). . . .

4.25a Appellations of origin (Not Mandatory before January 1, 1983).

(a) *Definition.* (1) *American wine.* An American appellation of origin is: (i) The United States; (ii) a State; (iii) two or no more than three States which are all contiguous; (iv) a county (which must be identified with the word "county", in the same size of type, and in letters as conspicuous as the name of the county); (v) two or no more than three counties in the same States; or (vi) a viticultural area (as defined in paragraph (e) of this section). (2) *Imported wine.* An appellation of origin for imported wine is: (i) A country; (ii) a state, province, territory, or similar political subdivision of a country equivalent to a state or county; or (iii) a viticultural area.

(b) *Qualification.* (1) *American Wine.* An American wine is entitled to an appellation of origin other than a multicounty or multistate appellation or a viticultural area, if: (i) At least 75 percent of the wine is derived from fruit or agricultural products grown in the appellation area indicated; (ii) it has been fully finished (except for cellar treatment pursuant to 4.22(c), and blending which does not result in an alteration of class or type under 4.22(b) in the United States, if labeled "American", or, if labeled with a State appellation, within the labeled State or an adjacent State; or if labeled with a county appellation, within the State in which the labeled county is located; and (iii) it conforms to the laws and regulations of the named appellation area governing the composition, method of manufacture, and designation of wines made in such place. (2) *Imported wine.* An imported wine is entitled to an appellation of origin other than a viticultural area if: (i) At least 75 percent of the wine is derived from fruit or agricultural products grown in the area indicated by the appellation of origin; and (ii) the wine conforms to the requirements of the foreign laws and regulations governing the composition, method of production, and designation of wines made in such country, province, etc. as appropriate. . . .

(e) (2) *Establishment of American viticultural areas.* Petitions for establishment of American viticultural areas may be made to the director by any interested party, pursuant to the provisions of 71.41(c) of this title. The petition may be in the form of a letter, and should contain the following information: (i) Evidence that the name of the viticultural area is locally and/or nationally known as referring to the area specified in the application; (ii) historical or current evidence that the boundaries of the viticultural area are as specified in the application; (iii) evidence relating to the geographical features (climate, soil, elevation, physical features, etc.) which distinguish the viticultural features of the proposed area from surrounding areas; (iv) the specific boundaries of the viticultural area, based on features which can be found on U.S. Geological Survey (U.S.G.S.) maps of the largest applicable scale; and (v) a copy of the appropriate U.S.G.S. map with the boundaries prominently marked. (3) *Requirements for use.* A wine may be labeled with a viticultural area appellation if: (i) The appellation has been approved under part 9 of this title or by the appropriate foreign government; (ii) not less than 85 percent of the wine is derived from grapes grown within the boundaries of the viticultural area; (iii) in the case of American wine it has been fully finished within the State or one of the States, within which the labeled viticultural area is located (except for cellar treatment pursuant to 4.22(c), and blending which does not result in an alteration of class or type under 4.22(b); and (iv) it conforms to the laws and regulations of all the State contained in the viticultural area.

4.26 Estate bottled (not Mandatory before January 1, 1983).

(a) *Conditions for use.* The term "Estate bottled" may be used by a bottling winery on a wine label only if the wine is labeled with a viticultural area appellation of origin and the bottling appellation of origin and the bottling winery: (1) is located in the labeled viticultural area; (2)

grew all of the grapes used to make the wine on land owned or controlled by the winery within the boundaries of the labeled viticultural area; (3) crushed the grapes, fermented the resulting must, and finished, aged, and bottled the wine in a continuous process (the wine at no time having left the premises of the bottling winery).

(b) *Special rule for cooperatives.* Grapes grown by members of a cooperative bottling winery are considered grown by the bottling winery.

(c) *Definition of "Controlled."* For purposes of this section, "Controlled by" refers to property on which the bottling winery has the legal right to perform, and does perform, all of the acts common to viticulture under the terms of a lease or similar agreement of at least 3 years duration.

(d) *Use of other terms.* No term other than "Estate bottled" may be used on a label to indicate combined growing and bottling conditions.

4.27 Vintage wine.

(a) *General.* Vintage wine is wine labeled with the year of harvest of the grapes and made in accordance with the standards prescribed in classes 1, 2, or 3 of 4.21. At least 95 percent of the wine must have been derived from grapes harvested in the labeled calendar year, and the wine must be labeled with an appellation of origin other than a country (which does not qualify for vintage labeling). The appellation shall be shown in direct conjunction with the designation required by 4.32(a) (2), in the same size of type, and in lettering as conspicuous as that designation. In no event may the quantity of wine removed from the producing winery, under labels bearing a vintage date, exceed the volume of vintage wine produced in that winery during the year indicated by the vintage date.

(b) *American wine.* A permittee who produced and bottled or packed the wine, or a person other than the producer who repackaged the wine in containers of 5 liters (or 1-gallon before January 1, 1979) or less may show the year of vintage upon the label if the person possesses appropriate records from the producer substantiating the year of vintage and the appellation of origin; and if the wine is made in compliance with the provisions of paragraph (a) of this section.

(c) *Imported wine.* Imported wine may bear a vintage date if: (1) It is made in compliance with the provisions of paragraph (a) of this section; (2) it is bottled in containers of 5 liters (or 1-gallon before January 1, 1979) or less prior to importation, or bottled in the United States from the original container of the product (showing a vintage date); (3) if the invoice is accompanied by, or the American bottler possesses, a certificate issued by a duly authorized official of the country of origin (if the country of origin authorizes the issuance of such certificates) certifying that the wine is of the vintage shown, that the laws of the country regulate the appearance of vintage dates upon the labels of wine produced for consumption within the country of origin, that the wine has been produced in conformity with those laws, and that the wine would be entitled to bear the vintage date if it had been sold within the country of origin.

4.32 Mandatory label information.

(a) Except as otherwise provided in paragraph (c) of this section, there shall be stated on the brand label:

... (c) In the case of imported wine, the name and address of the importer (when required to be shown) need not be stated upon the brand label if it is stated upon any other label affixed to the container. In the case of American wine bottled or packed for a retailer or other person under a private brand, the name and address of the bottler or packer need not be stated upon the brand label if the name and address of the person for whom bottled or packed appears upon the brand label, and the name and address of the bottler or packer is stated upon any other label affixed to the container.

4.34 Class and type.

... in the case of still grape wine there may appear, in lieu of the class designation, any grape-type designation, semigeneric geographic type designation, or geographic distinctive designation, to which the wine may be entitled. In the case of champagne, or crackling wines, the type designation "champagne" or "crackling wine" ("petillant wine," "frizzante wine") may appear in lieu of the class designation "sparkling wine." In the case of wine which has a total solids content of more than 17 grams per 100 cubic centimeters the words "extra sweet," "specially sweetened," "specially sweet" or "sweetened with excess sugar" shall be stated as a part of the class and type designation. The last of these quoted phrases shall appear where required by part 240 of this title on wines sweetened with sugar in excess of the maximum quantities specified in such regulations. If the class of the wine is not defined in sub-part C, a truthful and adequate statement of composition shall appear upon the brand label of the product in lieu of a class designation. In addition to the mandatory designation for the wine, there may be stated a distinctive or fanciful name, or a designation in accordance with trade understanding. All parts of the designation of the wine, whether mandatory or optional, shall be in direct conjunction and in lettering substantially of the same size and kind.

(b) An appellation of origin, such as "American," "California," "Napa Valley," or "Chilean," disclosing the true place of origin of the wine, shall appear in direct conjunction with, in the same size of type, and in lettering as conspicuous as the class and type designation if (1) a grape type (varietal) with geographical significance is used, or after December 31, 1982, any grape type used, under the provisions of 4.23a; (2) a semigeneric type designation is employed as the type designation of the wine, pursuant to 4.24(b); or (3) a brand name or product name qualified with the word "Brand" as required by the provisions of 4.39 (i) or (j).

4.35 Name and address.

(a) *American wine.* On labels on containers of American wine, there shall be stated the name of the bottler or packer and the place where bottled or packed (or until January 1, 1983, in lieu of such place the principal place of business of the bottler or packer if in the same State where the wine was bottled or packed, and, if bottled or packed on bonded premises, the ATF registry number of such premises) immediately preceded by the words "bottled by" or "packed by" except that:

(c) *Form of address.* The "place" stated shall be the post office address (after December 31, 1982 the post office address shall be the address shown on the basic permit or other qualifying document of the premises at which the operations took place; and there shall be shown the address for each operation which is designated on the label. An example of such use would be "Produced at Gilroy, Calif., and bottled at San Mateo, Calif., by XYZ winery, BW-CA-10001."), except that the street address may be omitted. No additional places or addresses shall be stated for the same person unless (1) such person is actively engaged in the conduct of an additional bona fide and actual alcoholic beverage business at such additional place or address, and (2) the label also contains in direct conjunction therewith, appropriate descriptive material indicating the function occurring at such additional place or address in connection with the particular product.

(d) *Trade or operating names.* The trade or operating name of any person appearing upon any label shall be identical with a name appearing on his or her basic permit or notice. In addition, after December 31, 1982, the registry number of the American bonded winery, bonded wine cellar, taxpaid wine bottling house, or distilled spirits plant at which the wine was bottled shall be shown on the label in direct conjunction with the name and address of the bottler, in type as conspicuous as the name and address.

4.39 Prohibited practices.

(a) *Statements on labels.* (2) Any statement that is disparaging of a competitor's products. . . . (5) Any statement, design, device, or representation of or relating to any guaranty, irrespective of falsity, which the Director finds to be likely to mislead the consumer. Enforceable money-back guarantees are not prohibited. . . . (9) Any word in the brand name or class and type designation which is the name of a distilled spirits product or which simulates, imitates, or creates the impression that the wine so labeled is, or is similar to, any product customarily made with a distilled spirits base. Examples of such words are: "Manhattan," "Martini," and "Daiquiri" in a class and type designation or brand name of a wine cocktail; "Cuba Libre," "Zombie," and "Collins" in a class and type designation or brand name of a wine specialty or wine highball; "creme," "cream," "de," or "of" when used in conjunction with "menthe," "mint," or "cacao" in a class and type designation or a brand name of a mint or chocolate-flavored wine specialty. . . .

(b) Statement of age. No statement of age or representation relative to age (including words or devices in any brand name or mark) shall be made except (1) for vintage wine, in accordance with the provisions of 4.27; (2) references relating to methods of wine production involving storage or aging in accordance with 4.38(f); or (3) use of the word "old" as part of a brand name.

V: ANNOTATED BIBLIOGRAPHY

This is a list of personal favorites, not a comprehensive guide and not at all specific to jug wines. Books on wine tend to age poorly, not only because they describe objects that no longer exist (a 1970 Mayacamas Cabernet), but because they can never quite keep up with a fast-changing art and industry. Those that endure are *books* first and *books about wine* second. Any of the following are worth having around to add to your enjoyment of everyday wines, and I've listed them in order of utility—from the practical to the poetic:

The Wines of America, Leon D. Adams. New York: McGraw Hill, 1978. This second edition of a worthy classic tells the story of wineries and the people behind them, rather than of specific wines. As of this writing it is the most comprehensive account of the industry, paying due respect to the products of Canada and Mexico as well as to the 700 vintners in 23 states. There is little here about selecting, serving, and tasting wine—for that was covered in the author's excellent primer, *Commonsense Book of Wine.* But this loving and accurate history is as useful as it is entertaining in bringing the wine buff behind the scenes.

Wines—Their Sensory Evaluation, Maynard Amerine and Edward Roessler. San Francisco: Freeman, 1976. Professor Emeritus of Enology at the University of California at Davis, Dr. Amerine is the author or coauthor of numerous treatises on wine that bear the definitive stamp of the scholar. Many are quite technical, but here the world-renowned authority takes a very subjective subject by the horns and has fun with it. If you are serious about the 20-points grading system used in most wine tastings, or simply want to acquire a better taste for fine wines, no other book can serve you as well. Every wine critic in the country should be required to pass a simple test proposed at the end of the book: to distinguish between two lists of words commonly used to describe wines—those that have specific meaning and those that are snares and delusions. Example: in the latter category are "nose" and "depth," as well as "voluptuous" and "silken."

There are many excellent compendiums of the worldwide wine scene, but one wonders how any of them could serve as more than reference or coffee-table books. Perhaps the fullest is Alexis Lichine's *New Encyclopedia of Wines and Spirits* (New York: Alfred A. Knopf, 1974). The array of beautiful photographs in this and similar tomes presents a strange contrast to its deadpan marshalling of detail. Hugh Johnson's *The World Atlas of Wine* (New York: Simon & Shuster, 1971) is more appropriate for one embarking on a tour with steamer trunks, and the writing is equally leisurely and sumptuous. *The Joys of Wine* (New York: Harry Abrams, 1975) is a mammoth joint effort of writers and photographers, in which romanticism begins to escalate. Anything by Frank Schoonmaker and André Simon is quite OK.

For those interested in specific regions, it shouldn't be difficult to find a book or two devoted to French, German, Italian, and Spanish wines; in this country books on California wineries abound. Norman Chroman has the best picture book, tasting evaluation, and history of the national scene in *The Treasury of American Wines* (New York: Rutledge-Crown, 1973); but so much has changed since then and a book this ambitious can hardly be turned out every few years. California dominates the book to the extent that it is probably misnamed. Sunset Books' *California Wines*, 1974, edited by Bob Thompson, is definitely a poor relation, but also knowledgeable and quite a bit less expensive. Thompson, the wine critic for *The San Francisco Examiner,* has collaborated with Hugh Johnson on the most impressive effort devoted to the golden state, *The California Wine Book* (New York: W. R. Morrow, 1976), a match for any of the international books mentioned above. The Pacific Northwest receives long overdue attention in *Winemakers of the Northwest,* Elizabeth Purser and Lawrence Allen (Seattle: Harbor House, 1977), another of the art-book type: most of us will have to wait for them to reach the remainder table. Quite a bit simpler but also a welcome relief from books on French and California regions is *Jefferson and Wine*, an historical exploration by the Vinifera Wine Growers Association, The Plains, Virginia (1976).

Now we begin to move to wine-talk as literature. The first new idea I have seen in a wine book in years is Robert Benson's *Great Winemakers of California* (Capra Press, 1976), aptly subtitled "Conversations with Robert Benson." Mr. Benson talks plainly with a score or more of the best wine makers in the state, without benefit of a public relations intermediary. They tell how they do it, and they disagree! The interlocutor also has the good sense to recommend a particular wine to be drunk while reading each interview—there's audience participation for you! Those who still believe that science will one day take the art out of wine making, take heed.

The finest piece of bookwork I've come across in this field is the limited edition, *The Great Wine Grapes and the Wines They Make,* obviously a labor of love (Great Wine Grapes, Inc., 1977), text by Bern Ramey. This is the Audubon book of the wine field, a magnificent example of taste and craftsmanship in typography, photography, and book production. Even at $37.50 and with highly selective information, this is good value.

The poets of the vineyard are surely the English. There's some sort of symbiotic relationship between the care that the British devote to small matters and the subtleties of fine wine. There may have been historical inevitabilities in the English devotion to the clarets of Bordeaux and the ports of Oporto (the Norman kings, the boycott by Napoleon), but I would rather believe that their gravitation to these two finest examples of viticulture are just another example of the civilized touch in human affairs. At any rate, Alec Waugh, Harry Waugh, Hugh Johnson, and H. Warner Allen immediately come to mind when wine appreciation in the grand manner is discussed. Ford Madox Ford indulged a fondness for long anecdotes revolving around the selection of a particular vintage, without being supercilious. In *Provence* he relates one incident in which he could easily have been fooled into accepting a young local wine as a famous vintage: he had been drinking champagne with lunch at the insistence of a generous stranger the day before ("Champagne may be all very well in its place—but I do not know what may be its place. ... Perhaps at a very young child's birthday party with an iced cake, or after two, at a dance, as a before-supper cocktail. ..."). A grasping cellarmaster had observed this gaffe and tried to pass off a refilled bottle as 1914 Château Pavie. Fortunately, part of the new cork lodged in the neck of the bottle and exposed the attempted fraud. The point of Ford's story, though, is that he was not sure he would have detected the inferior wine—even with all his experience of that region and vintage! "Who can really pledge his personal taste," he asks, "against such overwhelming things as the cork and bottle of the Château? Not I!"

This sort of approach to a book on wine—the raconteur's—is the hallmark of the Waughs and Allen. André Simon's classic *The History of Champagne* (London: Octopus Books Limited, 1971) is also in this manner. I heartily recommend Harry Waugh's *Diary of a Winetaster* (New York: Quadrangle Books, 1972), Alec Waugh's *In Praise of Wine* (New York: W. R. Morrow, 1959), and the elegant *The Romance of Wine* (New York: E. P. Dutton, 1932, now available in a Dover paperback, 1971), by H. Warner Allen. You won't find a guide to California jugs in any of these, but you will find the words that can connect what we now take for granted, in our everyday wines, with their noble ancestors.

General Index

Numbers in italic indicate illustrations

Acampo, 47
Acid level, 65
Aeration, 74, 114
Aging, 61ff., 74, 99, 114–15
Ahlgren, 96
Alatera Vineyards, 89
Alcoholic, definition of an, 109
Alexander Valley Vineyards, 85
Alfonso Rege, 53
Alicante, 54
Allen, H. Warner, 52, 58, 103, 104, 105, 115
Allen, Woody, 17
Almaden, 18, 22, *25*, 32, 33, 40ff., 52, 61, 69, 76, 78, 79, 80, 95
Almondoro, 68
Alvera, Paolo, 92
Amador Winery, 95
Amarine, Dr. Maynard, 20
Ambermint, 68
Ancient Mariner, 65
Angelica, 68
Aquino, 82
Argonaut Winery, 95
Aristophanes, 80
Arvin, 45, 64
Astor House, 45
Auslese, 39
Australian wines, 70–71

Bakersfield, 45, 64
Blazer, Robert Lawrence, 32, 42, 53
Bandiera Wines, 89
Barbera, 108
Barengo, 35, 52, 59, 79, 96
Bargetto, 52, 96

Baroque Burgundy, 58
Bear Mountain, 96
Beaulieu Private Reserve, 16
Beaulieu Vineyards, 13, *23*, 89, 93, 114
Bella Napoli, 92
Belloc, Hilaire, 111, 114
Benmarl Vineyards, 102
Beringer, *23*, 33, 61, 69, 79, 89, 93
Bertero, 52, 55, 85, 96
Bierce, Ambrose, 73, 74
Black Muscat, 68
Blind tastings, 46
Bocuse, Paul, 108
Boeger Winery, 87, 95
Bordeaux, 15, 48, 66, 73, 111
Borra's Cellar, 92
Bottles Up, 17
Bouquet, 53ff.
Breckenridge Cellars, 58
Brix, 52
Bronco Winery, 37, 64, 66, 79, 92
Bronson, William, 53
Brotherhood Winery, 100, 102
Bruce, David, 96
Buckley, Peter, 30
Buena Vista Winery, 13, 74, 102
Bully Hill, 24
Bureau of Alcohol, Tobacco, and Firearms, 32
Burger grape, 40
Burgess Cellars, 85, 88
Burgundy (region), 15, 48, 57, 68, 73, 111
Burgundy (type), 14ff., 20, 24, 47ff., 56ff.

Cabernet Blanc, 15, 60

Cabernet, Rosé of, 66
Cabernet Sauvignon, 15ff., 54, 56ff., 60, 65, 70ff., 91, 93, 99, 108
Caen, Herb, 12
Caldwell, Erskine, 27
Cakebread Cellars, 85
Calera, 96
California Growers (see Growers)
California Wine Association, 36, 55, 64 (see also Perelli-Minetti)
California Wine Institute, Technical Committee, 27, 39
Cambiaso, 35
Carafe, 75
Carey, Governor Hugh, 24
Carey, Richard, Winery, 91
Cargoes, 68
Carignane, 15, 24, 48, 50, 54
Carlo Rossi, 37
Cassayre-Forni Cellars, 89
Catawba, 24, 102
Caymus Vineyards, 85, 89
CC Vineyards, 66
Ceres, 47, 54, 64, 66
Chablis (type), 13ff., 24, 27, 34ff., 39, 49, 50, 106
Chalone, 85, 96
Champagne, 67, 70, 101, 104, 112
Champagne marathon, 96
Charbono, 54
Chardonnay, 39, 93, 99
Charles Krug (see Krug, Charles)
Chart Houses, 79
Chateau Chevalier, 85
Château Lafite-Rothschild, 55, 114
Chateau LaSalle, 65
Chateau Montelena, 85, 93
Chateau St. Jean, 39, 85
Chenin Blanc, 13, 15, 20, 34, 43, 49, 70, 93, 97
Cherry, Fred, 17, 47, 54, 66, 72, 99
Chesterton, G.K., 47
Cheval Blanc, 14
Chianti, 51
Chispa Cellars, 95
Christian Brothers, The, 22, 23, 29, 56, 58, 69, 76, 80, 81, 87, 89
Cider Song, A, 47
Claiborne, Craig, 106
Claret, 15, 20, 48ff., 56ff.
Clos du Val, 85

Coburn-Thorpe, Peter, 38
Coca Cola Company, 32, 44, 90
Cocktails, 104ff.
Coleridge, Samuel Taylor, 65
Colony (see Italian Swiss Colony)
Concannon Vineyards, 46, 71, 91
Concord, 24, 65, 102
Congress Springs, 96
Conn Greek Vineyards, 85
Consumer Reports, 55
Consumnes River Vineyards, 95
Corks and other closures, 21, 111, 113, 115
Country Wine, 66
Crawford, Charles, 19, 40
Cream Marsala, 68
Cresta Blanca, 34, 69 80, 81, 88
Cribari, 36, 53, 54, 64, 67, 79, 80, 81, 96 (see also Guild)
Cribari, Albert, 54, 65
Cuvaison, 85, 93
Cygnet, 96

D'Agostini, 11, 35, 58, 65, 95
D'Anjou, 60
Davis Bynum Winery, 85
Delano, 47, 64
Delicato, 36, 64, 80, 81, 92
Devil's Dictionary, 73
Diablo Vista Winery, 91
DiGiorgio, 11, 45, 64, 96
Domaine Chandon, 90
Dom Perignon, 47, 101, 111, 112
Don Juan, 37
Dosage, 104
Dreyfus, Alfred, 117
Dry Creek Winery, 89
Dry Sack, 69
Dry versus sweet wines, 24ff., 38 (see also sweet wines)
Durney Vineyards, 97

East Side Winery, 92
Ecclesiastes, 63
Edmeades Winery, 88
El Dorado Vineyards, 95
Eleven Cellars, 55
Elk Grove, 65
Ellegic acid, 110
Emerald Dry, 18, 33, 40
Emile's, 36, 75, 81
Enz, 96

Ernie's, 35
Exley, Frederick, 80

Falernian, 38, 104
Famiglia Cribari, 36, 53 (see also Cribari)
Farewell to Arms, A, 11
Farm Workers Pure Country Burgundy, 55
Farnesi Vineyards, 96
Felton-Empire Vineyards, 96
Ferara Winery, 97
Fetzer, 13, 22, 30, 50, 70, 79, 88
Field, James Arthur, 35
Field Stone Winery, 89
Filippi, J., 97
Fin de Nuit, 68
Finger Lakes region, 87, 102
Finigan, Robert, 51, 55
Fior di California, 82
Firestone Vineyards, The, 85, 97
Flavor of wines, 18, 103
Foods with wines, 105ff.
Foppiano, 36, 52, 59, 65, 78, 82, 88
Fortino, 82, 96
Foxy taste, 102
Franciscan, 50
Franzia, 11, 34, 37, 44, 61, 64, 66, 78, 92, 93
Frascati, 11
Freemark Abbey, 89, 93
French Colombard, 15ff., 20, 34
French wines, comparison with American, 55ff.
Fresno, 64
Frick, 96
Fruit wines, 68ff.
Fusco, Salvatore C. J., 12

Gallo, 11, 19, 22, 25, 31, 32, 33, 37, 40ff., 53, 55, 61ff., 64, 66, 69, 78, 79, 92ff., 115, 116
Gallo, Ernest and Julio, 93
Gallup, 38
Gamay, 15, 108
Gambarelli & Davitto, 82
Gemello Winery, 85, 96, 97
Generics, 15, 79
Gewürztraminer, 15, 39
Geyser Peak, 65, 78
Gibson, 65, 92
Gilroy, 61, 84
Giretti, 84, 90
Giumarra, 11, 36, 45, 58, 64, 79, 96
Gold Country, 58

Grand Cru Vineyards, 89
Grand Pacific Vineyard, 90
Grand Vefour, 105
Grape varieties, 15, 23ff.
Grapes of Wrath, The, 56
Great Day D-r-ry Sherry, 69
Great Western Wine Company, 70, 80, 102
Greeks, the, 14
Green Hungarian, 15, 45
Grenache, 15, 54, 60, 97
Grgich Hills Cellars, 85
Growers, 36, 45ff., 58, 64, 81 (see also Setrakian)
Guasti, 11, 34, 36, 44ff., 80
Guglielmo, Emile, 36
Guild Wines, 40, 64, 71, 78
Gundlach-Bundschu, 85, 87

Hacienda, 89, 102
Hallcrest, 96
Hanzell, 85
Haraszthy, Arpad, 73, 74
Harrington's, 81
Harvest, 64
Harvey's Bristol Cream, 14, 69
Haut Brion, 114
Health and wine, 109
Healdsburg, 65
Hearty Burgundy, Gallo, 37, 48, 53, 55ff.
Hecker Pass, 96
Heitz, 89
Hemingway, Ernest, 11
Henry VIII, 111
High Tor, 102
History of Champagne, The, 101
Hoffman Mountain Ranch Vineyard, 97
Homer, 38
Hop Kiln Winery, 85
Horace, 38, 104
How to Make Wine Like My Grandfather Did in Italy, 69
Hudson, Hudson Valley, 87, 99
Hudson Valley Wine Company, 101, 102
Husch, 88
Hybrids, 29

Imported wines, 18, 77, 79
Inglenook (Navalle), 29, 31, 32, 43, 49, 69, 76, 78, 79, 81, 89, 114
Iron Pot, The, 81

Italian Swiss Colony, 31ff., 42, 57ff., 79, 88
Ivie, Robert, 40

JFJ Winery, 37, 61, 79, 92
Johnson, Hugh, 65
Johnson, Samuel, 102
Johnson's Alexander Valley Winery, 89
Journal of Enology and Viticulture, 107
Judge's Secret Cream Sherry, 69

Keenan, Robert, 89
King Tut's Legacy, 108
Kirigan, 96
Kornell, Hans, 89
Krug, Charles, 13, 22, 23, 78
Kruse, Thomas, 96

Lambert Ridge, 89
Lambrusco, 14, 25
La Mesa, 64
Landmark Vineyard, 89
La Purissima, 96
Las Tablas, 97
Lautrec *(see* Toulouse-Lautrec)
Le Domaine, 70
Liebfraumilch, 40
Live Oaks, 96
Livermore Valley, 54, 71
Livingston Cream Sherry, 69, 107
Llords & Elwood, 69
Lodi, 64
Loire Valley wines, 29ff.
London Wine Bar, The, 82
Los Alamos Winery, 97
Los Angeles, 64
Los Angeles County Fair, 45, 58, 61, 62, 85, 95
Los Angeles Times, The, 32
Los Hermanos, 33, 51, 61, 79
Lost Hills Vineyards, 70
Louis Martini, *(see* Martini, Louis)

Macy's, 64
Madeira Port, 68
Magnums, 21, 71, 113
Malvasia Bianca, 24, 68, 69
Manor, 79
Manteca, 64
Marinades, marinating, 67, 103
Mark West Vineyards, 89
Martin Ray, 96

Martini and Prati, 89
Martini and Rossi, 69
Martini, Louis, 12, 39, 52, 78, 81, 82, 89
Masefield, John, 68
Masson, Paul, 18, 25, 28, 32, 41, 51, 58, 59ff., 61, 69, 78, 81, 93, 95
Mayacamas, 85
Mayer, Jean, 38
May wine, 69, 104
Mazzoni, Giuseppe, 89
Mencken, H. L., 115
Mendocino Country, 54
Merlot, 48
Metric system, 21
Milano Winery, 88
Mill Creek Vineyard, 89
Mirassou, 78
Mission San Jose, 91
Modesto, 64
Mogen David Wine Corporation 25, 26
Mondavi, C. K., 27, 30, 31, 32, 37, 42ff., 51, 58, 59, 61, 78, 81, 89
Mondavi, Robert, 13, 22, 30, 55, 57, 59, 70, 89
Monterey County, 33, 54
Monterey Peninsula Winery, 96
Monterey Vineyard, The, 93
Monteviña, 95
Morris, J. W., Port Works, 91
Mountain Castle, 63, 67, 114
Mountain wines, 27ff.
Mount Eden, 96
Mount Palomar Winery, 97
Mulled wine, 104
Muscadel, 29
Muscadelle du Bordelaise, 68
Muscadine, 48
Muscat, 65
Muscat Canelli, 68
Muscatel, 65
Muscat Frontignon, 65
Muscato amabile, 24, 65, 69

Napa Valley, 88
National Register of Historic Places, 87
Navalle (Inglenook), 32, 33, 43, 49ff., 56, 59, 61
Navarro Vineyards, 88
Nestlé, 31
New wine, 59, 66
New York Times, The, 35

Nicasio, 96
Nichelini, 89
Nonini, A., Winery, 96
North Coast Region, 58, 88, 96, 97

Oak, 26, 99
Oak Barrel Winery, 90
Obester Winery, 91
Old Man and the Sea, The, 117
Oliver, Raymond, 105
One-Upmanship, 59
Opici, 82
Orsini, 82

Pacific Southwest Airlines, 44
Page Mill Winery, 96
Papagni, 96
Parducci, 34, 52, 61, 79, 88, 99
Parducci, John, 26, 99
Pastori Winery, 89
Paul Masson (see Masson, Paul)
Pedrizetti, 96
Pedroncelli, 11, 34, 52, 79, 88
Perelli-Minetti, 36, 47, 64, 96
Petite Sirah (Syrah), 15, 48, 71
Petri, 11, 36, 96
Phelps, Joseph, 35, 93
Phylloxera, 73, 111
Pinoni, Pietro, 69, 108
Pinot Chardonnay, 15, 27, 41, 61 (see also
    Chardonnay)
Pinot Noir, 15, 24, 57, 71
Pliny the Elder, 105
Plymouth, 57
Pope Valley Winery, 89
Potter, Stephen, 59, 60, 75
Prial, Frank J., 56, 62
Private Guide to Wines, 51

Rafanelli, A., Winery, 89
Ramos Gin Fizz, 105
Rancho Sisquoc Winery, 97
Rapazzini, 61, 96
Raymond Vineyard and Cellar, 89
Red Mountain, 64
Red Table Wine, 57, 59
Rege, 53
Rhine Castle, 41
Rhineskeller Moselle, 43
Rhine type, 13ff., 37ff.
Riboli, 97

Rice, William, 38
Richert & Sons, 96
Rickel, Harry, 115
Ridge Vineyards, 85, 96
Riesling, 15, 34
Rioja, 70
Ripon, 64
Robert Mondavi (see Mondavi, Robert)
Roma, 11
Romance of Wine, The, 103
Romano, 82
Romans, 104, 105, 115, 116
Rosé, 58, 59ff.
Rosé of Cabernet, 60
Rosé of Zinfandel, 60
Roudon-Smith, 96
Round Hill, 89
Royal Winery, 101, 102
Rubion Claret, 51
Ruby Cabernet, 48, 52, 57
Rustico, 54
Rutherford Vintners, 89

Sacramento-San Joaquin Valley, 74
Safeway Stores, 63
Saintsbury, George, 104, 109
San Antonio, 21, 64, 76, 97
San Benito, 65
Sancerre, 29ff., 117
San Francisco, 64
San Francisco Chronicle, The, 12, 27
Sangria, 69, 104
San Martin, 36, 61, 93, 96
San Pasqual Vineyards, 97
Santa Barbara, 97
Santa Cruz Mountains, 96
Santa Inez Winery, 97
Santo Tomas, 97
Sauterne, Sauternes, 14
Sauvignon Blanc, 15, 43
Schoeppler, Wolfgang, 97
Schoonmaker, Frank, 75
Schramsberg, 85, 87
Sebastiani, 11, 31, 32, 62, 70, 71, 78, 79, 80,
    87, 93, 102
Sebastiani, August, Sam. J., and Samuele, 62
Sequoia, 92
Serving wine, 113
Setrakian, 45ff., 70, 96, 112
Setrakian, Robert, Scott, 46ff.
Shenandoah Valley Vineyards, 95

Sherrill Cellars, 96
Sherry de Oro, 68
Sierra Vista, 95
Silverado Squatters, 87
Simi, 88
Simon, André, 101
Smith-Madrone, 89
Smothers, Tommy, 39
Soave Bolla, 80
Sommelier Vineyards, 96
Sonoma, 74, 88, 102
Sonoma Vineyards, 29, 89
Sotoyome Winery, 89
South African wines, 70–71
Souverain, 70, 78, 90, 93
Spaetlese, 39
Spañada, 69, 103
Spritzer, 104
Stag's Leap, 85
Stanners, Jerry, 47
Steinbeck, John, 56
Sterling, 30, 32, 90
Stevenson, Robert Louis, 84, 87
Stonegate, 89
Stony Hill, 85
Stony Ridge, 92, 95
Stouffer's, 79
Sugar, addition to wine, 66
    reading (brix), 52
Summit, 34, 78
Sunrise, 96
Supermarket wines, 64ff.
Sutter Home, 24, 89
Sutter, Captain John, 95
Sutton, Denver, 53
Sweet vs. dry wines, 14, 18, 24ff., 38, 108ff.
Sweetwater Springs A Thousand Flowers, 85
Sycamore Creek, 96

Tadich Grill, 67
Taitinger, 112
Taste, sensations of, 26
Tavel, 60
Tavola, 66
Taylor, Walter, 24
Taylor Wine Company, 32ff., 41, 56, 61, 70,
    78, 96
Temperature of wine, 109
TGIF, 79
Trefethen, 85
Thierry, Ray, 66

Thompson Seedless, 27, 34, 37, 40, 65
Thunderbird, 65, 103
Thurber, James, 72
Tinta Madeira Port, 68
Toscani, 82
To the Lighthouse, 106
Toulouse-Lautrec, 60, 68, 71, 72, 106
Trader Vic, 101
Trentadue, 89
Tribuno Wines, 79
Triple Cream Sherry, 68, 69
Tulocay, 89

Ullage, 116
University of California at Davis, 16, 20, 36,
    60, 93, 107
University of Missouri, 110

Valley of the Moon, 35, 52, 81
Varietals, 15
Veedercrest, 39, 91
Vegetal character, 54
Viano, Conrad, 91
Victoria Stations, 79
Villa Armando, 54, 91
Villa Mt. Eden, 89
Vina Vista, 89
Vineburg, 47
Vinegar, 67, 116
Vino da Tavola, 66
Vin ordinaire, 19, 24
Vintage dating, 56
Vintner's Choice, 66ff.
Vitis vinifera, 65, 73

Washington Post, The, 32, 36, 38
Weibel, 13, 34, 88, 91, 112
Wente, 91
Whites vs. reds, 37ff., 117
Widmer, 102
Willow Creek Vineyards, 88
Windows on the World, 79
Wine and the People, 90–91
Wine consumption, per capita, 77
Wine is the Best Medicine, 110
Wine labels, California, 35
Winemaking, 56ff., 99ff.
Winemasters, 34, 71, 78, 92
Wine tastings, 14, 15, 16ff., 60
Wine Steward, 14
Wittwer Winery, 88

Women's preferences in wine, 37ff.
Wooden Valley Winery, 89
Woodland, 48
Woodside Vineyards, 96
Woolf, Virginia, 106

Yankee Hill Winery, 95
Yettem, 47, 64

York Mountain Winery, 97
Yosemite Road, 37, 44, 54
Yverdon, 89

Zinfandel, 15, 20, 48, 49, 51, 70, 85, 108
Zinfandel Blanc, 60
Zinfandel, Nectar of, 15
Zola, Emile, 117